God's Eternal Purpose

Unveiling Man's True Design!

Rudi Louw

The Holy Scriptures are just that, HOLY.

Statements enclosed in brackets were inserted into Scripture quotations to add emphasis or clarify to the meaning of what is being said in those scriptures. The integrity of God's Word to Man was not compromised in any way. Due care and diligence were cautiously exercised to keep the Word of Truth intact.

For example, the apostle Paul said in his second letter to Timothy in Chapter Three, Verse Sixteen that, *"All Scripture is given by inspiration of God* (literally God breathed), *and is profitable for doctrine, for reproof, for correction, for instruction **in righteousness."*** NKJV

Table of Contents

The Marvel of the Holy Bible

1. Uninterrupted Theme and Inspired Thought

It took *1,500 years* to compile the Holy Bible, involving *more than 40 different authors*. Yet the theme and inspired thought of Scripture continues *uninterrupted* from author to author, from beginning till end.

2. Absence of Mythical Stories

Compare philosophies and theories about creation in the Middle East, Europe, Asia, Africa, and Latin America and you'll find mythical scenarios: gods feuding and cutting up other gods to form the heavens and the earth, etc.

In ancient Greek mythology, Atlas carries the earth on his shoulders. In India, Hindus believe eight elephants carry the earth on their backs.

But in contrast, Job, the oldest book in the Holy Bible, declares that, *"God suspends the earth on nothing."* (Job 26:7)

This was said millennia before Isaac Newton discovered the invisible laws of gravity that delicately balance every planet and sun in its individual circuit.

In sharp contrast to every other ancient attempt to give a creation account, *the Holy Bible pictures the creation of the earth in a very scientific manner.*

For example: In Genesis Chapter One, the continents are lifted from the seas, then vegetation is formed and later animal life, all reproducing *'according to its own kind',* **thus recognizing the fixed genetic laws.** In addition, we have the bringing forth of man and woman, *all done by God in a dignified and proper manner, without mythological adornments.*

The balance or remainder of the Holy Bible follows suite.

The narratives are **true historical documents***, faithfully reflecting society and culture* **as history and archaeology would discover them thousands of years later. Not only is the Holy Bible historically accurate, it is also reliable when it deals with scientifically proven subjects.**

It was never intended to be a textbook on history, science, mathematics, or medicine. *However, when its writers touch on these subjects,* **they often state facts that scientific advancement would not reveal, or**

6

even consider, until thousands of years later.

While many have doubted the accuracy of the Holy Bible, time and continued research have consistently demonstrated that the Word of God is better informed than its critics.

3. Intactness

Of all the ancient works of substantial size, *the Holy Bible survives intact, against all odds and expectations.*

Compared with other ancient writings, the Holy Bible has more manuscripts as evidence to support it than any ten pieces of classical literature combined!

The plays of William Shakespeare, for instance, were written about four hundred years ago, after the invention of the printing press. Many of his original writings and words have been lost in numerous sections, *yet the Holy Bible's uncanny preservation has weathered thousands of years of wars, contradictions, persecutions, fires and invasions.*

Through the centuries Jewish scribes have preserved the Holy Bible's Old Covenant text, **such as no other manuscripts have ever been preserved. They kept tabs on every letter, syllable, word and paragraph.** *They* *continued from generation to generation to appoint and train special groups of men within their culture* **whose sole duty it was to preserve and transmit these documents <u>with perfect accuracy and fidelity</u>.**

Who ever bothered to count the letters, syllables, or words of Plato, Aristotle, or Seneca for that matter?

When it comes to the New Testament, the actual number of preserved manuscripts is so great that it becomes overwhelming. *There are more than 5,680 Greek manuscripts, more than 10,000 Latin Vulgate manuscripts and at least 9,300 other versions. Further still, there exists an additional 25,000 manuscript copies of portions of the New Testament.* **No other document of antiquity even begins to approach such numbers.**

The closest in comparison is Homer's <u>Iliad</u>, with only 643 manuscripts. The first complete work of Homer only dates back to the 13th century.

4. Unmatched Accuracy in Predictive Foretelling

The Holy Bible is unmatched in accuracy in predictive foretelling. No other ancient work succeeds in this, or even begins to attempt this.

Other books such as the Koran, the Book of Mormon, and parts of the Veda claim divine inspiration; *but none of these books contain predictive foretelling.*

This one undeniable fact we know for certain: *While microscopic scrutiny would show up the imperfections, blemishes, and defects of any work of man, <u>it magnifies the beauties and perfection of God</u>. Just as every flower displays in accurate detail the reflection and perfection of beauty, <u>so does the Word of Truth when it is scrutinized</u>.*

Historian Philip Schaff wrote:

*"Without money and weapons, Jesus the Christ conquered more millions than Alexander, Caesar, Muhammad, and Napoleon. Without science and learning, He (Jesus the Christ) shed more light on things human and divine than all philosophers and scholars combined. Without the eloquence of schools, He (Jesus the Christ) spoke such words of life as was never spoken before or since and produced effects which lie beyond the reach of orator or poet. Without writing a single line, He (Jesus the Christ) set more pens in motion and furnished themes for more sermons, orations, discussions, learned volumes, works of art, and songs of praise **than the whole army of great men of ancient and modern times combined**."* (*The Person of Christ*, p33. 1913)

Today, there are literally billions of Bibles in more than 2,000 languages.

Isn't it about time you find out what it really has to say?

Hey listen, the Holy Bible is all about Jesus, the Messiah, the Christ...

...and everything about Jesus Christ is really about YOU!!

Study Tips:

Read 2 Corinthians 5:14, 16, 18, 19, and 21.

In the light of these Scriptures, it should be obvious that, if you want to study the Holy Bible, *you should study it in the light of Mankind's redemption!*

Feed daily on **redemption realities** found in the book of Acts, in Romans Chapters One through Eight, and in Ephesians, Colossians, and Galatians. These realities are also found in 1 Peter Chapter One, 2 Peter Chapter One, James Chapter One, as well as in 1 and 2 Corinthians.

Foreword

Thank you for taking the time to read this book.

Let me start off by saying that *I am totally addicted to my Daddy's love for me.*

I am in love with Jesus Christ, *and that is enough for me!*

The love of God is so much more than a doctrine, a philosophy, or a theory. It is so much more and goes so much deeper than knowledge; *it way surpasses knowledge. **We are talking heart language here.***

Thus, I write *to impact people's hearts,* to make them see the mysteries that have been hidden in Father God's heart concerning Christ Jesus, and actually *concerning THEM,* so as to arrest their conscience with it, *that I may introduce them to their original design and to their true selves,* **and present them to themselves perfect in Christ Jesus** *and set them apart unto Him **in love**,* as a chaste virgin.

We are involved with the biggest romance of the ages. Therefore this book cannot be read as you would a novel: *casually.* It is not a cleverly devised little myth or fable. **It contains revelation and *truth* into some things you may or may not have considered before.**

**It is *the TRUTH of God, ultimate TRUTH,
and therefore has direct bearing upon
YOUR life.* The Word and the Spirit are my
witness *to the reality of these things!***

Be like the people of Berea the apostle Paul
ministered to in Acts 17:11. Open yourself up
to study the revelation contained in this book
***to discover for yourself the reality of these
things***.

*Be forewarned! Do not become guilty of the
sins of the Pharisees,* ***or you too will miss
out on the depth of fulfillment God Himself,
who is LOVE, wants to give you***.

Jesus said of the Pharisees and Sadducees
that they strain out every little gnat BUT
swallow whole camels. What He meant by that
is that *some people seem to have it all
together when it comes to doctrine and they
love to argue.* ***It makes them feel important,
but it is nothing other than EMPTY religious
and intellectual pride.*** *They know the
Scriptures in and out, and YET they are still so
IGNORANT about* **REAL TRUTH that is only
found in LOVE.** They are always arguing over
the use of *every little jot and tittle* and over the
meaning and interpretation of **every word of
Scripture,** *but they are still so ignorant and
indifferent* **towards the things that REALLY
MATTER!**

The exact thing they accuse everyone else of
doing though, the precise thing they judge

everyone else for, *they are actually doing themselves.* That is **they often downright misinterpret and twist what is being said, *making a big deal of insignificant things while obscuring or weakening God's real truth: the truth of His LOVE.*** *They are always majoring on minors* **<u>because they do not understand the heart of God</u> and therefore they constantly miss the whole point of the message.**

Paul himself said it so beautifully,

"...the letter kills but **the Spirit BRINGS LIFE;"**

"...<u>knowledge puffs up</u>, but **LOVE EDIFIES.***"*

I say again: *Allow yourself to get caught up in the revelation I am about to share.* Open yourself up to study the insight contained in this book, *not only with a desire to gain knowledge, but also with anticipation* **to hear from Father God yourself; to encounter Him through His Word, and to embrace truth, in order to know and believe the LOVE God has for <u>you</u>, and get so caught up in it, that you too may receive from Him LOVES' impartation of LIFE.**

The message proclaimed in the gospel and thus also revealed in this book is the voice and call of LOVE Himself to every human being on the face of this earth. *If you take heed to it, it is custom designed and guaranteed to forever alter and enrich your life!*

Acknowledgment

I want to acknowledge and thank one of my mentors in the faith, Francois du Toit, for blessing and impacting me with revelation knowledge.

I borrowed the portion on *"The Marvel of the Holy Bible"* from his website: http://www.MirrorWord.net, as students so often feel they have a right to do with things that come from teachers they respect. Just as Galatians 6:6 says, *"Let him who is taught the Word **share in all good things** with him who teaches."*

To all our dear friends and family, for all the love and support, and to Chase Aderhold and all those who helped me with this project:

THANK YOU!

Also, especially to my wife, Carmen;

For keeping me real by being my companion in life and partner in ministry,

I love and appreciate you so very much!

"Eye has not seen, nor ear heard, nor have entered into the heart of Man

the things which God has prepared
for those who love Him.

Now we have received,
not the spirit of the world,

but the Spirit who is from God,

that we might know the things

that have been freely given to us
by God."

These things **we also impart,**

not in words which Man's
wisdom teaches

but with words
which the Holy Spirit teaches,

combining Spirit with spirit.

For who has known the mind of
the Lord
**so as to be knitted together with
Him?**

But we have the mind of Christ"
1Corinthians 2:9 -16

Chapter 1

God Has Canceled All Distance

Isaiah 43:10-13,

10 *"You are My witnesses,' says the Lord, 'and My servants whom I have chosen, that you may know and believe Me, and understand that I am He. Before Me there is no other God, nor can there be a replacement for Me."*

11 *"I, even I, am the Lord, and besides Me there is no savior."*

12 *"I have declared and saved, I have proclaimed, and there was no foreign god among you; therefore you are My witnesses,' says the Lord, 'that I am God.'"*

13 *"Indeed before the day was, I am; and there is no one who can deliver out of My hand; I work, and who will reverse it?"*

Indeed we are God's witnesses. God is speaking *to us the believers* right now as those who have seen that they are indeed His kids, His people, the Church, His Temple, *those in whom He dwells, the very manifest fullness of God upon the earth right now. Our faith, our very existence as Children of God upon this earth proves that He alone is God.* He declared it from the beginning and then He brought it to pass in Jesus, *and He's deposited that life inside of us, by that very Word in our hearing, and in our embrace of it.*

And so, what we are going to discover, and are already busy discovering right now, is that, *God is revealing inside of us the fullness of everything He's done in Christ Jesus.* We are discovering in His Word, in Jesus, and in the gospel, *who we are, and what God has done.*

I want you to know that there's coming the mightiest release of the children of God that has ever existed on the face of this earth.

We have sat long enough in religious shackles with the darkness of the enemy blinding our minds *to the glorious truth of what God has unveiled and done* in Christ Jesus ...**but God is revealing it.**

I believe that this is the day, the very hour; it is time for us to partake of everything that God has already unveiled and done for us.

Hallelujah!

In the book of Acts, when Paul was getting ready to leave the city of Ephesus, he called the brethren together before heading towards Jerusalem, and in his final goodbye to them he said (Acts 20:32),

32 *"And now brethren, **I commend you to God <u>and to the Word of His grace</u>, which is able to build you up and give you an inheritance among all those who are sanctified.**"*

In this book we are going to be commending ourselves *"<u>to the Word of His grace</u>",* (the Word of the revelation of Jesus Christ) and I believe *it's going to build you up.* It's going to edify you, *it's going to open up your understanding,* bless your spirit, *expand your life, and it's going to cause you to enter in and enjoy the fullness of God.* It's going to cause you to become that which you've always dreamed and known inside your spirit that you should and could be.

Listen, God has not created us to polish a pew with our blessed assurances, amen?!

Hallelujah!

God has called us to be a mobilized people and there's nothing that's going to motivate you and mobilize you like *"the Word of His grace.*" It is the only thing that can *successfully* cause us to be proper ambassadors of God our Father; **the revelation of Christ in us is the hope of glory.**

So I want to encourage you to do what the apostle Peter has to say in 2 Peter 1:19,

21

19 *"…you would do well to take heed* **to this Word** *as a light that shines in a dark place,* **until the day dawns and the morning star rises in your own hearts***;"*

Peter actually starts his letter off by saying in 2 Peter 1:2,

2 *"Grace and peace* **be multiplied to you through the full knowledge of God,***"*

He was saying in actual fact that,

"Grace (**the favor of God; the release of God's power on your behalf**) *and peace* (**an unbroken fellowship with Him**)*;"*

*"…***be multiplied to you;***"*

*"…***through the full knowledge of Him***."*

This then is also my whole purpose in writing this book: *That this mystery about God and us and the life that has been hidden becomes revealed, so that we may all enter into it and enjoy it and rejoice in it with the Father.*

I want us to come to *an appreciation of* **the reality** *of the fact that God* **has brought us together** *in Him and that* **He has canceled distance***.*

What a revelation!

God has brought us together in Him, and by so doing, *He canceled distance.*

You know, God's geography is so different from ours. He says in Ephesians 2:13 that, *"... we who were afar off,* (far apart, He brought us nigh,) *He brought us near, to Himself* (and to one another,) *by the blood of Christ."*

He brought us into that place of common witness through *"the Word of His grace",* by His Spirit, *into a place of friendship and fellowship* **that is far richer** than what we could ever express through any formal structure of a meeting, or through any formal religious ritual, or any formal organization mentality, like a big corporation in the business world. Even if it is a non-profit organization, even if it is a church, it can so easily get so stiff and formal and impersonal, ***outside of a thorough understanding and clear revelation into these new creation realities.***

And you see that corporate or business mentality ends up robbing us **of the richness of friendship and fellowship that is ours in Christ Jesus.**

Romans 12:1 & 2 clearly tells us *not to be conformed to this world,* to worldly thinking and the worldly wisdom of this world; *not even the corporate business wisdom of this world.*

That worldly wisdom is foolishness to God! *It is foolishness when it comes to the spiritual household; the family God is building!*

I am not saying that that wisdom of the corporate business world cannot be used *to*

23

benefit us some in the administrative business side of ministry, **but we cannot afford to allow that corporate business mentality to come into our fellowship with one another.**

We must make **a clear distinction** between that wisdom, *and being the family of God,* **or it will rob us of that richness of friendship and fellowship God has in mind for us.**

God in His wisdom *has called us to friendship and fellowship. He has called us into His family,* **to be a family, and not a business.**

He didn't have a corporation in mind when He called His children out of the darkness this world walks in, into the family of God, amen!

It is my prayer that we as the body of Christ, as the dwelling-place of God *will come to understanding, and like PRECIOUS faith, and thus love,* **and truly appreciate one another in Him.** *God has called us into the richness of friendship and fellowship.* **He has brought us together in Him and He has canceled all distance!**

If it wasn't for the gospel contained in it, the Scriptures would hold no meaning! So, I'm going to be sharing with you from this wonderful document, the Holy Scriptures, because of the Word of God, because of the gospel it contains, *so we can just appreciate together God's full deposit in us.* I want us to allow Him to so stir and awaken our hearts in Him.

24

Prayer

Father, we thank you for the living and abiding Word; for its eternal impact in our lives!

I thank you for Your ability to engrave upon our understanding, TRUTH, *which not even contradiction can erase.*

We thank you Father for the eyes of our understanding being *enlightened,* as we behold together, *as we gaze together, into this marvelous, perfect, law of liberty.*

We thank you that *this liberty is ours,* that it's meant for us, that You saw it for us, *that You saw us included in the release You proclaimed through your Son's resurrection,* when You introduced in the earth, a new species, a new Man, *a new humanity.*

We thank you that we may *boldly discover and declare our union with You* in Christ Jesus.

We've found our lives *hid with Christ in God.*

Hallelujah!

Thank you Father. We honor You right now in our praise.

We honor You as we worship You, Your Majesty.

We thank you that You call us, *to be eye witnesses, of the majesty of God* …the One who said, "*Let light shine out of darkness*" … *the very One responsible for shining into our hearts* **the light of the knowledge of the glory of God,** *which You revealed and wanted us to see, and comprehend, in the face of Christ.*

We thank you, Father, *for such glory,* in Jesus' name.

Chapter 2

Before The Ages, God Decreed

It is so wonderful to discover the Word of God, not as a manual, *but as Emanuel (as God with us, face to face with us, as God present, His presence is here with us)*. Not as some new handbook with a new set of rules, you know, re-adjusted because the first commandments were a little bit above our ability to keep, so God just re-adjusted the Word a little bit to make it more possible for us. As if *He introduced a new commandment,* you know, **a new set of rules,** *which still leaves us to the frustration of our own effort.* But no, *it's so wonderful to discover this legal document, the gospel,* **as revealing our legal release.**

I saw a translation from John Chapter 1, Verse 1 the other day, you know that Scripture that says,

1 *"In the beginning was the Word, and the Word was with God, and the Word was God."*

This one translation says,

1 *"...**In the beginning was the Word, face to face with God**..."*

Hallelujah! That's what we've come to discover, *a face-to-face encounter with God, a face-to-face encounter in His Word, a face-to-face encounter of Him, of His thoughts, **of His Word concerning Man,** in Christ Jesus.*

If you would, turn with me in your own Bible to 1 Corinthians Chapter 2 to begin with, and let's read Verse 7. If you don't have access to your Bible right now, then just keep reading (I'm reading from the *Revised Standard Version*).

1 Corinthians 2:7,

7 *"But we impart a secret and hidden wisdom of God, **which God decreed before the ages, for our glorification**."*

*"...**which God decreed before the ages**..."*

I'm so glad that God **had His mind made up** before the ages, before time or human history or any human experience was there *to contradict what He thought and what He decreed.*

God had His mind made up.

He had it *settled* in His heart. He saw by faith a being, invisible then, but **a being *who would visibly accommodate His glory, and visibly emanate and reveal all that was to be known of an invisible God.***

And so it says in that Scripture,

*"…before the ages **God decreed** **Man's glorification**…"*

Did you know that **the Gospel** *is the revelation* **of Man's worth? It's the revelation** of how God saw a being, *standing in the full radiance of His own invisible beauty.*

And it says there in Verse 7 that,

*"…**we** **impart** **this wisdom and hidden secret**…"*

It's wonderful to be the audience and the recipient of life-impartation, of TRUTH-impartation, *that brings a liberty beyond **our** **own definitions** of life and truth.*

You know, sometimes we in the so called, *"Church"* become so formal in our definition of life, *that we forget to **live.***

But when TRUTH is *imparted,* a new knowledge comes to our hearts, *which dawns within us a new day, and* awakens our understanding to **the understanding of God,** and *sets our thinking free from any limitation, from any boundary we have allowed **through our past experience.***

Paul says,

*"…**we** **impart this**…"*

Sometimes we think that *insight and revelation* is something *so profound* **and so far beyond**

us *that it's going to take many days and many seasons* **before we finally attain to some small level** *of understanding.* But Paul makes it *so simple* in Ephesians Chapter 3 and Verse 2.

He says in Ephesians 3:2,

2 *"While you read this, you will perceive my insight, into the mystery of God."*

"While you read this..."

"...you will perceive..."

God does not have in mind a mystery *beyond our reach.* He never hid things *from Man,* but **instead He hid them for Man.** God doesn't have in mind *a confused Church.*

So relax Max,

Hallelujah! Ha... ha... ha...

Praise God, **God has insight in mind for us!** *He has life changing insight in mind, for every individual,* **and it's not beyond our reach.** It's not way off in South Africa somewhere, and it's not way over here in America either!

Hallelujah, **it's near unto us**.

Paul says,

"While you read this ...you will perceive my insight..."

30

He invites us *to enjoy the same "**insight**" that* *introduces us to the same encounter.*

Listen, insight is not there to add to our definitions, and our theology and our philosophy and our manuscripts. <u>Insight is there *to add to our encounter of Him*, *to release our encounter of Him*</u>!

Knowledge has no worth outside of that release! Everything loses its value outside of that encounter!

1 Corinthians 2:7,

7 *"**We impart** a secret and hidden wisdom of God, **which God decreed**..."*

Now when the Bible speaks of God, decreeing something, *it speaks of a God who has His mind made up to such a degree that He is not going to be interrupted.*

God says in Isaiah 43:13,

13 *"...I will work **and who can hinder Me?**"* or

*"...I work, **and who will reverse it?**"*

Hallelujah!

God works and who can *hinder* Him? God is not about to *be sidetracked.* He is not about to *be distracted in His purpose.* ***God never needed to adjust the Word He spoke that was from the beginning,* even in spite of the**

Fall and all its gory details. He's not a God who's confused, *having to adjust His Word to changing times and seasons.*

God only spoke one Word, *and it was a final Word,* amen! **And the incarnation** *gives definition to that Word.*

1 Corinthians 2:7,

7 *"...**God decreed** before the ages..."*

When we're dealing with the Word of God, **we're dealing with God's decree,** *God's purpose, God's* **eternal** *purpose and plan* **revealed.** God saw in this decree, *Man's glorification.* "...**God decreed, before the ages,** *Man's glorification.*"

No wonder Job wrote and he said in Job 7:17,

17 *"What is Man* **that You make** **so much** *of* **him?"**

In other words, *'Come on God, look at Man, look at his failings, look at him in his sinfulness,* **how can You make so much of him?'**

God decreed something *before Man was* ...in the beginning when His Word was.

1 Corinthians 2:8,

8 *"...none of the rulers of this age understood this..."*

Hallelujah! So, even though God never hid this *from us* but **for us, He hid it from our enemy.**

"…none of the rulers of this age understood this;"

"…for if they had, they would never have crucified **the Lord of glory.**"

If they understood *that He was the lord* **of glory;** if they *had access* to the mystery of God, if they *could interpret* that mystery, *they never would have allowed the cross!*

1 Corinthians 2:9-10,

9 *"But as it is written: 'What no eye has seen, nor ear heard, nor the heart of Man imagined';* **What God has prepared for those who love Him, God has revealed to us, through the Spirit,** *for the Spirit searches everything, even the depth of God."*

There's a Scripture in Job that says (Job 11:7):

7 *"Who will know the limits of the Almighty?"*

"Can you find out **the deep things** *of God?"*

"Can you find out the limit (**the measure**) *of the Almighty?"*

The most popular answer to this question would be:

'Far out, man!'

*'No way, Jose. **Way out of reach!**'*

*'I mean, **we'll never get there,** so let's just continue to guess* about this magnificent majestic God.'

But God in His greatness *has no greater desire* ***than to accurately define His greatness!***

...And no, not in outer space somewhere, *but **in a being** that could so reflect, in communion and companionship, **His very own glory** that **that being, called Man,** would be **the full recipient** of that **which He saw within Himself, and declared him to be.***

Chapter 3

The Measure Of God

Jesus said in John 14:9,

9 *"If you've seen Me, <u>you've seen</u> the Father."*

That brought an end to the mystery of God's greatness.

Jesus gave measure to God's majesty. His life, His person, His ministry, His very purpose **gave measure to God's majesty.** *In the incarnation and work of redemption,* the great, omnipotent One, **measured His being,** in a work *every bit as great as He is!*

When Moses sings of Him in Deuteronomy Chapter 32, he says (Deuteronomy 32:3-4),

3 *"Ascribe greatness to our God, the Rock."*

4 *"**His work is perfect…**"*

And how the enemy sought for years *to separate,* in the mind of the religious Church, *God, from His work!* How we have enjoyed the goose-bumps, celebrating a great majestic God, a God who rules the universe, in our praise, **while at the same time belittling His**

workmanship. What an insult to Him that *we have belittled and thought little of His work.*

Ephesians 2:10,

10 *"For **we are** <u>His</u> workmanship, **created in Christ Jesus**..."*

*"...CREATED **IN** CHRIST JESUS unto good works."*

Jesus is the only mold that God had in mind for Man. *He is* the only blueprint, the only pattern, *the only measure* He ever had in mind for Man.

God never saw a being *that would be of lesser value in His person* to what God in His own being could see for Himself and for His Son.

He never saw a Man *who would stand in a lesser place than what His Son enjoys.*

In Genesis 1, the Scripture brings an end to that short-sighted theory about Man. He says in Genesis 1:26,

26 *"Let Us make Man **in our image, in our likeness."***

Let's allow this glory, this revelation, which God decreed, before the ages, about us, *to be imparted to us* ...to be **imparted!**

I love impartation of **love** and of **life,** *because it bypasses our reasoning,* **which can sometimes get in the way, and restrict us so much,** *from experiencing the full measure!*

1 Corinthians 2:10,

10 *"…for the Spirit searches (explores)* **the deep things of God***…"*

*"…***the depths of the Almighty.***"*

*"…***the measure of God.***"*

And He explores the depth of it, *for one reason, for one purpose:* **to communicate the deep things of God** <u>**to those who love Him**</u>**!**

1 Corinthians 2:11,

11 *"For what person* **knows a man's thoughts** *except the spirit of the man which is in him;"*

"…so also, no one comprehends **the thoughts of God,** *except the Spirit of God."*

BUT,

12 *"***Now we** <u>**have received**</u>*, not the spirit of the world, but the Spirit which is from God;"*

*"…***<u>so that we might understand the things bostowed upon us by God</u>***."*

God's desire for His Church, for us, and really, for the whole world, is **_to understand_ the things bestowed upon us by God.**

Hallelujah!

If the enemy *could interrupt,* if he *could **limit** or **distort our understanding** of **these things,*** *then he could **totally neutralize** our faith, and our life, and our ministry.*

But we *have received* the Spirit which is from God, so that *we may <u>understand</u>,* so that *we may enjoy <u>complete insight</u>* into the things *bestowed upon us* <u>by God</u>!

I know most translations, even the RSV says, *"...**gifts** bestowed upon us by God..."* But the original Greek says, *"...**things.**"* We might get into 2 Peter Chapter 1, where Peter speaks about *"**these things.**"* But for now let's go on reading here in 1 Corinthians Chapter 2.

1 Corinthians 2:13,

13 *"**And we impart <u>this</u>**..."*

What do we *impart?*

*"...**these things**..."*

...Interpreted; **understood by revelation, *by insight brought into our understanding.***

*"...**things**..."* which the heart of Man *could not,* **dared not** have imagined!

38

*"…**things**…"* which *the eye of Man* **could not see.**

*"…**things**…"* which the knowledge of Man *could not comprehend.*

*"…**these very things**…"*

*"…**we impart.**"*

You see the wisdom of this world, *kept Man imprisoned,* to an experience, to an identity, to a lifestyle, <u>less than what God originally designed for us</u>. The wisdom of this world, *the ability of this world to define life,* even in its wildest dreams, *was still a life inferior to the glory God decreed for Man to enjoy.* Man in his greatest ambition, *found himself imprisoned, to a life, <u>even in achievement of that ambition,</u>* he found himself imprisoned to a life that left him miserably disappointed and unfulfilled.

I met with a highly successful businessman in Greenville 2 or 3 weeks ago, and he had been listening to some of my CDs and reading some of my books. And this man was just beaming as he said to me,

'Rudi, you know what? I have lost all my ambition. Hallelujah!'

He said to me,

'I discovered life in its full measure.'

Amen, isn't that a wonderful testimony? **It's exactly what God** *has in mind for us:* **life in its full measure,** *no longer driven by empty ambition.* **Hallelujah!** ...*Life as He saw it,* **in His own imagination, when He conceived in His thoughts,** *a being that could be His* **companion.**

1 Corinthians 2:13,

13 *"...we impart this,* **in words**, *not taught by* **human wisdom** *..."*

"Human wisdom" remains limited to human experience, to human ambition, to human speculation. But, *"...we impart* **this** *..."*

"... **this** *reality..."*

"...these things the Spirit reveals..."
Because He **knows,** *because He has searched out* **the deep things of God!**

"... **we impart this in words** *..."*

"... **in words** *..."*

Hallelujah!

Praise God for *"**words**".*

"In the beginning was **the Word,** **face to face with God**."

As an artist would enjoy that canvas, and the color, and the brush in his hand, and see within that canvas, *the possibility, of **so communicating**, so expressing, **his thought, just so, God has seen, *in language, in words,* the vehicle, *to so contain, and to so reveal,* <u>all that He saw</u>, to such a degree that <u>*this Word*</u> will not leave us ignorant or desolate or cut off and confused, *but enlightened!***

1 Corinthians 2:13,

13 *"...**we impart <u>this</u>, in words,** not taught by human wisdom, but **taught by the Spirit**..."*

And then the RSV says,

*"...interpreting **spiritual truths,** to those who possess the Spirit."*

I like that word *"interpreting"* used there, but the original Greek word there is actually the word, *"**combining**".* It actually reads,

*"...**<u>combining</u> Spirit with spirit."***

You see it's not complicated. *"Interpreting"* might be a complicated thing, but he says,

*"...**we impart this, in words, <u>combining Spirit with spirit</u> (combining the Spirit of God with the spirit of Man)."***

41

In other words, <u>God is not going to keep this Word from the babes</u> *because it's just too complicated for them to understand.* **No, combining Spirit with spirit; even in the babes!**

You see, *"...None of the rulers of this world understood the cross..."*(1 Corinthians 2:8) But God understood it. And the Spirit *who knew* the heart of God, *who knew* the purpose, the mystery, *He reveals it,* He imparts it, <u>*heart to heart*</u>, even to the babes, *"...<u>combining Spirit with spirit</u>."*

He goes on to say in 1 Corinthians 2:14-16,

14 *"The unspiritual man* (or naturally oriented; naturally minded; natural identity minded and oriented Man) ***does not receive*** *the things of the Spirit of God."*

Why?

Not because he cannot *receive them,* not because *they are not available* to him, or because *he is not allowed to have them.*

NO!

He **cannot** receive them, *"...**for they are folly to him**, and he is not able to understand them, **because they are spiritually discerned,** (**and so he still prefers worldly wisdom and the wisdom of the flesh; he is holding on to his natural minded thinking and natural identity** ...**thinking as a mere Men!**)"*

15 *"The spiritual man judges* (discerns and understands, and becomes truly wise in) *all things, but he himself is to be judged* (enlightened or condemned) *by no one."*

16 *For '…who has known the mind of the Lord so as to instruct Him?'* (RSV)

*"For '…who has known the mind of the Lord **so as to be knitted together with Him**?"* it says literally in the original language.

I know the original Greek word used here can also be translated *"to instruct,"* but who is going to instruct God on anything? Listen, it's the same word used in Colossians 2:2 that says that our hearts are, *"…**knitted together** … through mutual understanding."*

So, it should properly be changed there in your Bibles to read,

*'…who has known the mind of the Lord **so as to be knitted together with Him**?'*

You see, Man used to think, *'How can we know and explore **the mind of God?** It's impossible.'* And oh how we love to quote the part of Isaiah 55, which says that, and I paraphrase (Isaiah 55:8-9),

8 *"…the thoughts of God are not our thoughts. The ways of God are not Man's ways."*

9 *"As the heavens are higher than the earth, so are God's thoughts higher than our thoughts, and His ways higher than our ways."*

"...Who has known the mind of the Lord?"

"...Who is able to explore the thinking of God?"

And then we hear God say in the next verse,

10 ***"But as the rain, and as the snow comes down from heaven, and communicates and imparts to the earth that life, which awakens the latent dormant seed, and transforms the face of the earth,"***

11 ***"so shall My Word be that goes forth from My mouth...***"

Go read it there for yourself and allow God to change the way you used to look at it. Allow God to bring new revelation and insight and understanding to what He is trying to communicate to the heart of Man in that Scripture.

People, I don't want us to underestimate *the value of God's Word, the worth, the treasure of the gospel, the wealth of this Word,*

*"...**so shall My Word be**...*"

Listen, God just desires to bring us into a place of *being the audience* of His Word.

"…When you read this …you will perceive …my insight…"

And then the last line of 1 Corinthians 2:16 says, *"…But we have the mind of Christ."*

In the Scriptures, in Jesus, in the work of redemption, we have *"the mind of Christ."*

1 Corinthians 2:16,

16 *"For '…who has known the mind of the Lord so as to be knitted together with Him?' … But we have the mind of Christ."*

Oh, that we may become *like-minded with God and be knitted together with Him.*

Then as we begin to enjoy *like-precious faith together with God,* we will *become like-minded with each other also* and *be knitted together with each other in love.*

Chapter 4

When God Speaks, Man Is His Theme

Quickly turn with me in your own Bible to Hebrews Chapter 1 and Verse 1, or just keep reading if you still don't have your Bible available.

Hebrews 1:1,

1 *"**In many and various ways God spoke** of old, to our fathers, by the prophets…"*

I am so glad that Man's fall *did not shut God up,* amen!? I mean if God would *stop speaking,* then that's it, the end, *all is lost.*

But Hebrews 1:1 says,

1 *"In many and various ways **God spoke** of old, **to our fathers, by the prophets**…"*

What was God's message to our fathers by the prophets? Would you agree *it was Man's redemption, Man's release?* I mean God's mind *is full of Man. He just cannot get Man off of His mind. Ha… ha… ha…* When God speaks, *Man is His theme,* because Man is the theme of God's thought-life. When God thinks, *He thinks about Man.* Amen!?

You better believe it, because this Bible; the gospel it contains, wasn't written for angels, *it was written for Man, for <u>you</u>.* And not as a manual, *but as Emanuel (as God with us, God present, God communicating with us, face to face with us).*

Hallelujah!

The Bible was not given as some set of rules *that we should continue to try and attain to, but as a precious document, containing the* **revelation, *the gospel,* the receipt of our release, the revelation of Man's release.**

There's a large difference between a postdated check, a postdated promise, and *a receipt.*

And while we have the attitude of a promise that is yet to come, *we're just going to continue to wait for something that has come already!*

**But if this document, the New Testament, *is indeed a legal receipt of your release,* then you might as well believe it, because what God spoke to our fathers, what God spoke through the prophets, *and what God then revealed,* concerning *"this great salvation,"* He also *literally revealed and manifested and brought into reality and accomplishment* in Christ, *on your behalf, for you to enjoy and enter into!*

I'm so glad that the Bible calls it:

*"...this **great salvation**..."*

It wasn't a small little Mickey Mouse job *to release Man.* God accomplished that *through His divine power.* Through His divine ability, through His divine foresight and insight, His divine wisdom, **and His mighty LOVE, He accomplished our release!**

The apostles challenges us, *"…let us not **neglect** this great salvation."* Let us not *underestimate* and become *too familiar* in a negative sense of the word; let us not become *casual,* or *flippant,* **with this salvation. Let us not take for granted, a salvation *that totally qualifies us,* a redemption that qualifies *our release, that reveals our identity in our Father's opinion* …not on the basis of anything we could dream or imagine, but on the basis of *an eternal thought,* on the basis of *a final Word, revealed in a Son!*

This Word, which was from the beginning, *face to face with God, was about to speak face to face with Man.* And so in Verse 2 of Hebrews Chapter 1 it says,

2 *"…in these last days **He has spoken to us**…"*

Do you see that Man *is God's audience?* **Do you see that God has something to say to YOU?**

Hebrews 1:2,

2 *"…He has spoken **to us** …in the Son…"*

And there *in the full stature, in the majestic glory of God in a Man,* **there, in a Man; in the man, Jesus, the Christ,** God spoke to Man, face to face. **He spoke to us in** *a Son* (Hebrews 1:2),

2 *"...***whom He appointed the heir of all things***..."*

Do you see God's living epistle, God's man, standing before the human race, *being and declaring the Word of God, revealing and declaring all that the prophets spoke?* **Every promise of God,** *every intention of God with Man,* everything **God decreed,** *visibly revealed, and declared, in a Son,*

"...whom He appointed the heir of all things,"

*"...***through whom also He created the world***..."*

*"*We are **His workmanship,** *created* **in** *Christ Jesus..."*

...Not in the mold of human failure or human experience, but, "...created **IN** *Christ Jesus..."* (Ephesians 2:10)

Hebrews 1:3 says,

3 *"***He reflects the glory of God***..."*

(**A man**, *reflecting, exhibiting, radiating the* **glory of God.**)

"...He gives distinct visibility to an invisible God."

Hallelujah!

*"...and bears **the very stamp** of His nature..."*

*"...**the very stamp**..."*

*"...**of His nature**..."*

The Greek word there for *"**stamp**"* is the word, GARACTER, where we get our word **character** from. But it is a word also commonly used **to describe a tool *used for engraving something.*** You don't want to *engrave* something, *unless you want it to last,* unless you want it to say something *that would out-live all contradiction.* God *"**stamped**,"* He *"**ENGRAVED**"* His personality **in the flesh.** *He **ENGRAVED** His <u>love</u> and <u>truth</u> in human flesh!*

The incarnation is *the engraving* of the voice of God, **of the *eternal voice of God,* of His eternal involvement with Man.**

God *"**ENGRAVED**"* **His invisible being visibly** in the person of His Son. **Jesus stands *forever,* for *all eternity, as the* testimony of a God <u>*whose work is perfect*</u>, <u>as the testimony of God Himself</u>!**

Hebrews 1:3,

3 *"**He emanates the exact glory of God**..."*

He does not stand, as a man in the flesh, *inferior to the glory of God,* having a limited ability to communicate *the exact nature that he partakes of,* the very personality of *the God who is love* that he *represents* and *exhibits.*

3 *"He emanates the glory of God, **and bears <u>the very stamp</u> of His nature."***

Oh, can you grasp it?

John 1:1,

1 ***"In the beginning was the Word, face to face with God..."***

And now *"in these last days",* that same Word, *stands face to face before Man,* in Him.

Hebrews 1:3,

3 *"**He upholds the universe by the Word of His power...**"*

It must be **some Word** to be able to, **"up-hold the universe."** It means that the total universe *finds its place of significance* in this declaration of God, in this decree of God *revealed!*

When God decreed Man, He decreed a being *that would stand in equal glory to His own nature.* His image, His likeness, on display, **nothing less!**

What did sin rob Man of?

Romans 3:23,

23 *"…All have sinned and fallen short **of the glory of God**…"*

The word *"**glory**"* is such a rich word in its meaning.

In the Greek, it comes from the word: DOKAO and its root: DOXA, which means, **to *imagine*, or to *form* <u>an opinion</u>.** Now I would have you know that when God **forms an opinion**, it's not actually an opinion, per se. What I mean is that it's not just a mere opinion. God's opinion is **the truth!** Amen?!

So, *"…All have sinned and **fallen short of what God imagined**…"* or,

*"…All have sinned and fallen **away from the opinion of God**… "*

*"…from **what God knows to be truth**…"*

Listen, God's imagination, *His original design of Man,* <u>His truth concerning Man</u>, His opinion, *was reflected in the person of His Son,* and the whole universe is held together, upheld, *by His truth.* It's upheld by His mighty decree *that cannot be reversed,* by *His Word of power,* by *this mighty, powerful <u>Word</u>!*

And what did Jesus accomplish? The rest of Verse 3 says,

3 *"...**when He had made purification for our sins**..."*

It is compelling that *"**sins**"* should be mentioned **in this context *of truth,* this context *of God's glory, of God's image revealed in the flesh.***

Quite often people define the word SIN according to the Scripture that says that, *"sin is the breaking of God's Law."* But to more accurately understand what that means, we have to do a more thorough study of this word SIN, especially in this context of Hebrews *which mentions SIN **in the context of God's truth and glory,** of His image and likeness revealed in the flesh.**

The very word SIN is an old Anglo Saxon word and has the connotation of an archer aiming at a specific target, such as the bulls-eye on a larger target and shooting at it, *only to miss it.* In other words, to SIN literally means **TO MISS THE MARK.**

So, God's glory, *God's image and likeness revealed in the flesh,* is the exact mark, *the very truth* Man fell away from and falls short of. Thus, *falling short of that glory, falling short of God's truth, falling short of that image and likeness is what SIN is all about.*

God's truth, God's glory, God's image **revealed in the flesh** is **the essence** (the bulls-eye) **of *what Man fell short of,* *thus coming back to that truth and to that glory,***
54

to that opinion of God about us and its expression in our person and our lives is the essence of what it means to HIT the mark.

It is also interesting to note that the word for SIN in the New Testament is the word HAMARTIA or HAMARTANO, which literally means *to live outside of ones design,* **outside of what you were designed for.**

Thus to sin, by breaking the Law, means that *you are violating the Law of your design,* **you are violating** *the truth of it* **and are** <u>being deceived</u> *and missing the mark of accurate faith.* **You are** *not seeing. You are ignorant of,* **or worse yet, you are ignoring: You refuse to believe and yield to** *the truth of your design,* **and thus you are falling short** of it; *missing the mark of your design,* **violating the law of your design,** *violating your true identity and design, which the Law of Moses was only a shadow and a picture of.*

Hebrews 1:3,

3 *"...when He had made purification for sins,* <u>**He sat down**</u> **at the right hand of the Majesty on high,"**

Does that speak of Him **having accomplished something,** *amen!?* **He removed Sin. He removed the dominion and the government of the thing that caused Man to fall short** *of the glory of God, of the image of God*

55

revealed in the flesh, of Man's original design. He destroyed the very evidence that the enemy used to manipulate and blackmail the human race with.

Colossians 2:13-15 reveals that,

13 *"...having forgiven us of our sins,"*

14 *"He canceled the bond which stood against us with its legal demands"*

"...He nailed it to the cross."

Did you know that the living epistle of God's glory *became the letter, the legal document of our judgment, of our condemnation we lived under?* He the living epistle of God's glory therefore also became the letter, the legal document of our release! He was nailed to the cross. Against that cross was nailed, not a little formula, not a little letter, just a little Scripture or two, but against that cross was nailed *the whole Word of God!* Against that cross was nailed a man, a person, in the flesh, *the exact same flesh that sin staked its claim upon,* the exact same flesh that sin had its dominion over was nailed to that cross and by so doing *"He canceled the bond which stood against us with its legal demands..."*

And Verse 15 of Colossians 2 says that, *"...He thus disarmed principalities and powers..."*

Hebrews 1:3,

3 *"…**when He had made purification for sins**…"*

He, as God's epistle, as God's Word to Man, as the very reflection of God's glory, *was made sin.* He who knew no sin, *He who in His being knew no sin.* In His being, for all eternity, *He only knew the glory of God.* He had no knowledge beyond that. *His being could not exhibit anything less than the glory of God. He who knew not SIN,* **He became that bond which stood against us, He became** *that SIN document,* **He became that** *legal document,* **that document** *of deception and manipulation and sin, and accusation and guilt and shame,* **which the enemy used as his claim.**

If I carry with me *a document that qualifies my judgment* of another person, if I carry with me *some kind of legal evidence against* another individual, **then I could easily use that evidence as a tool** *to blackmail, deceive, or manipulate and control that person.* **I could use that evidence** *to have dominion over* **another. And this is exactly what the enemy managed to do to Man.**

Through one man's offense, *through Adam's embrace of the lie,* **through his own questioning of truth within himself,** through Adam's self-deception and opening himself up to deception, ***through that SIN*** *that came into* *the world, that initial introduction to it,* to Adam and through Adam, **sin and death came into power and spread to all Men.**

Thus through Adam's missing the mark, **through his falling away from his original design,** *the reign of sin was* <u>established</u> **and its effect came upon the whole human race!**

And Satan could *continue his cruel rule over Mankind* **through that initial agreement, that legal contract** between him and Adam, **that document of sin and guilt, and of condemnation and lying accusation,** *and outright deception.*

But **God the Father sent Jesus to come and demonstrate His truth and His love, and to save us** *from Satan's lies and deception!*

Jesus did not come to save Man *from God.* He came to save us *from Satan!* He came to save us from the father of lies and deception! He came to save us from ourselves, from our own self-delusion and the guilt, shame and condemnation we experience in ourselves as a result.

Romans 5:8, *"...**God demonstrated His own love towards us** in this, that while we were yet sinners, Christ died for us..."*

Hebrews 1:3, *"...**when He (Jesus)** **had made purification for sins**..."* *"...**He thus disarmed principalities and powers**."* - Colossians 2:15

58

God has never been our problem. The father of lies was our real problem. Lies and deception and confusion *were* **our problem.** But, Jesus came *"...**to give us understanding, so that we may no longer be confused about God,** but may indeed **know Him** who is true, and that we might also know that **we are in Him** who is true."* - 1John 5:20 **We are in His heart! We are in Him! We are on His mind all the time!**

Jesus came *to make the Father* **fully known!**

"He is the official authority qualified to announce God! God remained invisible to Man, until the authentic original, begotten only of God, until that Son, came and revealed Him. The One who is in the bosom of the Father, and represents that innermost being of God, came to unveil Him, and bring Him into full view!" - John 1:18, (Mirror Bible)

Hebrews 1:3,

3 *"...**when He** (**Jesus**) **had made purification for sins**..."*

*"...**He thus disarmed principalities and powers**."* (Colossians 2:15)

In that extravagant display of His love, He came and forgave and removed our trespasses, like a thick cloud which blocks the sun *is removed by the wind.* **He removed** *that wall of deception and sin and legal condemnation* **that separated Man from**

God, *and caused us to miss the mark* ...and caused us to fall short of the glory of God, <u>*of the image of God revealed in the flesh*</u>.

He, Jesus, *dealt with it* in His own person.

And now *He is* <u>*seated*</u> at the right hand of the Father.

This means *His work was done, it was accomplished successfully,* and thus *He is seated* at the right hand of God.

And this Word, this wisdom revealed, this gospel, *communicates our place in the Father,* in His heart ...it communicates our eternal identification in Him!

Let's read on.

Chapter 5

We Must Pay Closer Attention

Hebrews 1:14,

14 *"…Speaking about the angels: Are they not all ministering spirits sent forth to serve* **for the sake of those who are to obtain salvation?"**

They were serving us through the prophetic word, through visiting the fathers with dreams and visions and prophetic profound utterances, and they were sent forth as servants, *"…**for the sake of those who were to** <u>obtain</u> **salvation**."* God had nothing less than <u>salvation</u> in mind for ALL mankind.

Hebrews 1:7,

7 *"…Of the angels He says: 'Who makes the angels winds and His servants flames of fire…"*

Notice the word, *"…**servants.**"*

Verse 8 says,

8 *"But of the Son He says: 'Your throne,* **O God**, *is forever and ever…"*

He was referring to the Messiah, *the natural descendant of David; born of the lineage and genealogy of David.* **God calls that natural descendant of David, God calls a man, a human being,** *"God,"* here in this verse of Scripture, and in several others David prophesied in, which are quoted in this chapter of Hebrews and in the next.

To this Acts 2:30-33 and Romans 1:3 & 4 also bear witness:

Acts 2:29-33

29 *"Men and brethren let me speak freely to you of the patriarch David, that he is both dead and buried, and his tomb is with us to this day."*

30 *"Therefore, being a prophet, and knowing that God had sworn with an oath to him that **of the fruit of his own body, according to the flesh, He would raise up the Christ to sit on his** (David's) **throne,"***

31 *"he* **(David), *foreseeing this, spoke concerning the resurrection of the Christ,*** *that His soul was not left in Hades* (a place of darkness; the place of the dead), ***nor did His flesh see corruption*** (decay).*"*

32 *"**This man, Jesus, (the Christ) God has raised up,** of which we are all witnesses,"*

33 *"**Being exalted by the hand of God, to the right hand of God***…"*

Romans 1:3-4

3 *"…concerning His Son Jesus Christ our Lord,* **who was born <u>of the seed of David according to the flesh</u>,***"*

4 *"***and declared to be the Son of God,** *with power, according to the Spirit of Holiness, by the resurrection from the dead."*

Jesus Himself, *even after His resurrection,* said in John 20:17,

17 *"Jesus said to her, 'Do not cling to Me, for I have not yet ascended to My Father; but* **go to <u>My brethren</u>** *and say to them, I am ascending* **to My Father <u>and your Father</u>, and <u>to My God</u>** *and your God.'"*

This same apostle John who quoted Jesus here went on to say in 1 John 2:18,

18 *"Little children, it is the last hour; and as you have heard that antichrist is coming,* **even now many antichrists have come***…"*

In Chapter 4, Verses 1 to 3, he continues the discussion,

1 *"Beloved, do not believe every spirit, but test the spirits, whether they are of God; because many false prophets have gone out into the world."*

2 *"***By this you know the Spirit of God: Every spirit that confesses that Jesus Christ <u>HAS COME IN THE FLESH</u> is of God***,"*

3 *"and every spirit that does not confess **that Jesus Christ HAS COME IN THE FLESH** is not of God."*

*"And **this is** (this deception, this sheer misunderstanding concerning the identity of the Christ, **THIS IS**) **the spirit of antichrist, which you have heard was coming, but is now already in the world.**"*

Why is it so crucial *to understand **these things?*** Why is it so crucial **to understand that Jesus Christ *HAS COME IN THE FLESH* ...to understand that, even though this man was at one point 100% God, before the ages, *He left that glory?*** (John 17:5)

Why is it so vital to understand these things? To understand that **HE CAME IN THE FLESH. He laid aside that majesty and became 100% Man, *the man Jesus Christ.*** And not only that, but after he HAD COME IN THE FLESH, *after being made 100% Man, he died, and was raised again, and received up into Heaven.*

Through the resurrection from the dead, *a **glorified man** was received up into heaven itself, absorbed up into that unseen eternal realm of spirit reality, **to forever be again 100% God.***

Why is it so crucial **to understand** that Jesus Christ **HAS COME IN THE FLESH?**

Because it has everything to do *with US!*
64

It has everything to do *with our freedom from sin, as Man, as people, as individuals!* It deals with *every one of our excuses!* If he CAME IN THE FLESH, being 100% Man, *and overcame sin IN THE FLESH,* as a man, then we, being IN THE FLESH, being 100% Man, *can ALSO overcome sin IN THE FLESH, as regular ordinary people, because we are not ordinary, according to what is revealed in the incarnation,* and because of what is restored to us in full, in His work of redemption!

I say again: We can ALSO overcome sin IN THE FLESH *BECAUSE OF HIS WORK OF REDEMPTION!*

Romans 8:3 says,

3 *"For what the Law could not do, in that it was weak THROUGH THE FLESH, God DID,*

...by sending His own Son IN THE LIKENESS OF SINFUL FLESH, on account of sin:"

(To deal with the issue of sin, to deal with this thing called SIN, to deal with sin's hold over the flesh, and *to do away with it:*)

"...HE CONDEMNED SIN IN THE FLESH."

But let's go back to Hebrews Chapter 2:1,

1 *"Therefore __we must pay the closer attention to what we have heard, lest we drift away from it__."*

65

Did you know that it's possible to drift away from God's decree, *from God's declaration concerning you,* **from His truth revealed concerning you?**

Jesus reveals <u>you</u>! He reveals <u>*your*</u> *release,* <u>*your identity*</u>.

You are <u>God's workmanship</u> created in Him, *revealed.*

But it's possible to drift away from what you have heard, *from this Word God declares over you, concerning you.* It's possible to be enticed with another word, another gospel, a different gospel, *a different opinion, a word of weakness* that is like a little leaven, with a little emphasis on personal effort, *beyond the final Word.*

Hebrews 2:1,

1 *"Therefore* **<u>we must pay the closer attention to what we have heard,</u> lest we drift away from it."**

The principle of the parable of the sower *is actually just one principle, not many.* **It is the principle of HEARING.** At the end of the parable Jesus said (Luke 8:18),

18 *"Take head then <u>what you hear</u>…"*

Another translation says, *"Be careful <u>how you hear</u>…"*

He says (Luke 8:16),

16 *"…**After one light up a lamp** one would not place that lamp **under** a bed or **under** a bushel…"*

Did you know it is possible *to be once enlightened* and then to allow the bed, *the comfort-zone,* the religious rituals and traditions of men, the culture and customs you live in ...or the bushel, *some kind of business,* to come in and to dominate and *put under* subjection *that liberating word of enlightenment?* It's possible to allow that *"bed"* or that *"bushel"* to so destroy the evidence of that lamp, of that light, *of that which is being ignited in your spirit* ...so that all that God saw in Christ and declared concerning you, and said to you, *you drift away from*.

I've seen many precious believers excited in the Word, only to have *the first or the second contradiction wipe them out.*

God wants us to discover a Word *of such substance,* a Word that *so fully declares our release IN THE FLESH, that no contradiction would successfully diminish the impact of that Word upon our spirits!*

God does not expect our fellowship to be built or based upon a lesser word, *than the Word <u>that acknowledges every good thing that is in us in Christ Jesus</u>*. We are not to

reduce our conversation *to anything less, amen!?*

Paul says in 2 Corinthians Chapter 4, Verse 2 that,

2 *"I have renounced disgraceful ways. **I refuse to tamper with God's Word.**"*

Why Paul, why? Paul would answer back, *'Why **adjust** God's Word to a lesser experience, so as to **exalt that experience** **above God's Word** and then continue to **accommodate** that lesser experience?'*

*'Why **stretch** my doctrine, just a little bit, **to accommodate failure IN THE FLESH** when this Word exhibits **a redemption of perfection**, a redemption that **actually, totally, completely qualifies me already?'***

Hebrews 2:2-3,

2 *"For if the message declared by angels <u>was valid</u>, and every transgression and disobedience **received a just retribution**,"*

3 *"**how shall we escape**..."*

(From such just spiritual retribution and repercussions, from a lesser life trapped in a fleshly existence only, from the power AND WAGES of sin, from that kind of JUST RETRIBUTION)

3 *"how shall we escape* (from those things) *if we* (ignore, or) *neglect such a great salvation?"*

What is this Word that we are not to drift away from?

The gospel; "...__such a great salvation__..."

What does this *"__salvation__"* reveal? **Man's true identity, and Man's release IN THE FLESH.**

Let's read Verse 6,

6 *"It has been testified somewhere* (He is quoting Psalm 8 here) *saying,*

'What is Man that You are mindful of him **(that Your mind is full of him)?"'**

Here, David asked the very same question Job asked.

"...What is Man that You are so mind full of Him?"

"What is Man that You make so much of him?"

So David asks (Hebrews 2:6-7),

6 *'What is Man that You are mindful of him* **(that Your mind is full of him)?'**

*'Or the son of Man, **that You care for him?'***

69

7 *"You made him a little lower than **the angels**…"*

Now the Greek manuscript of this verse says, *"**angels**,"* but this quotation taken from Psalm 8 in the original Hebrew or Aramaic language doesn't say *"**angels**"* at all. The actual word used is the word ELOHIM. In other words, it should read,

"You have made him a little less than ELOHIM (which is the word used for **God Himself**)

So Hebrews 2:7 says,

7 *"You have made him a little less **than God Himself** …**You have crowned him with glory and honor**…"*

Why would God crown Man with glory and honor?

The word *"honor"* speaks of *God's estimation of your worth*.

If you honor someone, **you communicate that person's worth.**

*"…**You have crowned him with glory and honor**…"*

And so God *"crowns"* **the individual**...

God *"crowned"* every individual; God **crowns** **Man**…

70

Chapter 6

The Mystery Of The Gospel

God doesn't see Man as mere decoration on this planet. God sees Man as *the extension of His throne, He* sees him as His dominion in the earth revealed. He *"**crowns**"* him, not because He's just playing a game, or because He's just playing around with little crowns and crowning us to look nice, but He sees in that *"**crown**"* **His own person, *His own authority, revealed.***

Hebrews 2:8, *"…putting **everything in subjection under** his* (**Man's**) ***feet…"***

And here comes the commentary now from the author of Hebrews, *to clarify what is being said by this previous statement, so we can make no mistake about it **and misinterpret its meaning.***

It is almost as if he has dealt with Man's natural thinking before, **and knew what Man's response would be,** *so he wanted to make sure we don't tamper with the clarity of the previous statement.*

8 *"…Now in* **'putting <u>everything</u> in subjection to him ...He left <u>nothing OUTSIDE his control</u>…"**

If God puts <u>everything</u> in subjection <u>to Man</u>, then He does not see <u>anything</u> excluded from that authority.

8 *"…As it is, we do not yet see everything in subjection to him…"*

And so here comes the point of confusion in our theology, and so we read that Scripture and we think, *'Well, there we have it,'* and we develop a neat little theory called: **The Positional and the Vital, The Legal and the Experiential.**

'Oh yes, positionally, brother Rudi, we are there, but experientially we're far from it brother…'

'Legally, brother Rudi, we're there, but vitally we still have a long way to go to get there…'

'It is going to take at least another death, another crucifixion, before we get there, the crucifixion and the death of Self, brother Rudi…'

Listen acutely and carefully to me now. Tell me, **when and where did Self get crucified and die?** Let me put it another way: *Who died when Jesus died?*

I'm speaking now about *the mystery revealed.* **What was *the mystery* about His death? *Man's inclusion <u>there</u>!* That's *the mystery* of the Gospel.** That's *the power* of the

Gospel: **that Jesus did not die *an individual death*.**

That's what the rulers of this earth did not perceive. They did not comprehend the fact that <u>this one man's death, *represented the death of the whole Adamic race*</u>.

So we've given Man time and we've said, *'Well, we do not see it yet, but maybe in 4 months from now…'*

But Jesus, after He ministered to the woman at the well, He says to the audience, the town's people, who came out to see Him because of her testimony, He says (John 4:35),

35 *"Do you not say that, 'There are yet four months, and **then** comes the harvest?'"*

*"**But**,"* He says, *"I say unto you, **lift up your eyes**…"*

In other words, *"**Stop looking at the harvest from Man's point of view** …'Oh, you know, that person is not quite ready yet.'"*

When is the harvest ready?

When the seed <u>in the ear</u> *matches the seed that was sowed*.

In other words, **when the seed that is being sown, *brings forth a mature response, in the ear; <u>a matching faith</u> response, <u>in the heart</u> of the hearer*.**

73

So, the harvest is ready **when the heart of the hearer _fully_ embraces the seed** ...when the **soil responds** *positively* **to the seed that was sowed,** *and fully embraces that seed,* **and** *when the proper interaction happens, between that seed, and the soil.*

When the heart of the hearer _fully_ embraces the seed, that's when the harvest is ready! That's when true faith comes!

He says in John 4:35,

35 *"...But I say unto you,* **lift up your eyes***, the fields* **are _already white unto harvest_***!"*

Hebrews 2:8,

8 *"...**But***..."*

(Man's reasoning,)

"...as it is, we do not yet see everything subject..."

*"...**But***..."*

(Jesus' response to Man's reasoning,)

*"...**I say unto you** ...the fields* **are _already white unto harvest_***!"*

Hebrews 2:8,

8 *"...we do not yet see everything subject..."*

74

Let's read on in Hebrews 2:9,

9 *"**BUT** we see Jesus…"*

What do you see when you see Jesus? Jesus is the Word made flesh. So what is Jesus? Jesus is *God's voice to Man,* **God's living** *epistle,* **God's living** *legal document of Man's release.*

9 *"**BUT** we see Jesus…"*

If I'm going to continue to look at fallen Man as my testimony, *I will continue to have every excuse in the book* **to shrink from faith, to shrink from what the Word says, and I will continue to be intimidated,** *through my own up and down personal experience, as well as through* others' up and down personal experiences. **And I lose my confidence** *and don't make any progress.*

9 *"**BUT** we see Jesus…"*

You see, the Gospel *challenges our intelligence* **to see Jesus; to see ourselves in Jesus.**

1 Corinthians 2:16,

16 *"…We have the mind of Christ…"*

In these Scriptures, **we have the mind of Christ**.

Hebrews 2:9,

9 *"…and He, for a little while was* (also just like us) *made lower than the angels,* **but we see Him crowned with glory, and with honor,** (there goes our excuses out the door) *and through the suffering of death, and by the grace of God,* **He tasted death <u>for everyone</u>**.*"*

Hebrews 1:3,

3 *"…After having made purification for sin* **He <u>sat down</u>**…*"*

How do you see Jesus? Having accomplished our release! Having accomplished our redemption!

I do not see Jesus *as an excuse for my failure* (That is not what this Scripture or any other Scripture anywhere in the Word teaches about Jesus!) **I do not see Jesus** *as an excuse for my failure* **(That is not what the blood of Jesus is for)!**

Hebrews 2:8,

8 *"…***we do not yet see** (maybe in Heaven one day) *…***but as it is now,** (according to our own opinion, according to our experience) *we do not yet see Man's release,* **but** (at least, to comfort us in spite of our failure and weakness) **we see sweet Jesus** (we see a marvelous promise for the future, for one day in Heaven, **even though it isn't helping us much now**) …*"*

This is NOT what the Scriptures say!

76

We've interpreted it conveniently for years as such:

8 *"…we don't see Man, you know, there yet,* **but** *we see our Jesus…"* It's a wonderful excuse!

Listen, <u>God is not confused</u> when He looks at Christ. The suffering of His death, <u>was the grace of God revealed</u>, and *exercised on our behalf,* not an empty promise for somewhere off in the future! The grace of God is not an excuse for sin, *it is the precise work and power of God* by which we have been and are (practically, literally) *delivered from sin's hold on us.*

When Paul said in 1 Corinthians 15:10,

10 *"**By the grace of God <u>I am what I am</u>***…"

He wasn't making excuses saying, *'I am but a weakling, I am but a sinner saved by grace, I am but a failure in my walk as a Christian. But I'm still okay, because by the grace of God go I.'*

NO! He went on to say in 1 Corinthians 15:10,

10 *"…and **His grace towards me was not in vain**…"*

He was saying, **"<u>By the grace of God</u> *I am what I am,"*** *'And what am I **because of that grace**? What am I **by the grace of God**? What am I **by that grace?'** 'What am I?'*

77

'I am <u>a new creation</u>! I am <u>complete in Him</u>! I am no longer <u>a weakling</u>. Christ now is my life! <u>I am strengthened by His Spirit's indwelling and instruction</u> here in my inner man!'

*'I used to be a sinner, **but grace saved me**. I am no longer a sinner. I used to be one, but now I am that no longer.'*

'What am I?'

'<u>I am</u> what the Scriptures say I am, <u>I am</u> a new creation now. <u>I have been set free</u> from the power of sin, and because of <u>the gift</u> of righteousness, <u>I now reign in life</u> through the one, Christ Jesus.'

So the suffering of Christ's death <u>was the grace of God revealed</u>, *and exercised **to our practical benefit.***

When God looks at Christ, *He knows what He sees. He knows what happened in Him! He knows <u>what was accomplished</u> in Him!*

*I say again, **God is not confused when He looks at Christ. He knows that this one man's death, represented the practical death, of the whole Adamic race.***

We all died in Him!

And we were all raised to newness of life in Him!

Chapter 7

Bringing Many Sons To Glory

Hebrews 2:10,

10 *"…For it was **fitting, that He**…"*

*Because of **His decree** from before the ages,* because of the fact that **He has eternally linked Himself to Man in covenant commitment when He decreed** in Genesis, *"Let us make Man in our image, in our likeness." …Because of His decree from before the ages,* and because of *His association of us and with us in the eternal Word; in Christ Jesus;* because, *"**He chose us in Him** before the **Fall** (KATABALO) of the world …even before **the very foundations** of the earth!"*

*…**Because of that association and decree from before the ages,*** Hebrews 2:10 says that,

10 *"…**it was fit to make the pioneer of their salvation perfect through suffering**…"*

I want you to note that Jesus was not made perfect through suffering, but that **our salvation was perfected or completed through His suffering.**

Is Jesus **a perfect** <u>**pioneer**</u> *of a perfect salvation?* **Yes, He is!** Are we *"His workmanship?"* **Yes, we are!** **Amen!**

Deuteronomy 32:3-4,

3 *"Ascribe greatness to our God,"*

4 *"...**His work is perfect;**"*

His suffering, His obedience, the judgment which was our due, which He took upon Himself, *perfectly released us, perfectly restored us and reconciled us to Him.*

Hebrews 2:11,

11 *"...For both He who sanctifies and those* ***who are sanctified...**"*

Where are they *"**sanctified?**"*

In His death, in His suffering, in Him taking upon Himself that legal document of accusation and guilt and shame, *and canceling it.* We are *"**sanctified**"* in Him becoming Himself *a new legal document of innocence restored,* <u>thereby releasing us</u>!

He reintroduced that eternal decree; that eternal and legal document that is ironclad.

It is older and stronger than any other supposed legal contract and agreement between Adam and Satan any day!

Just like the Law, which was introduced 430 years after Abraham, **could not annul that covenant which God had already formerly made,** first on behalf of Adam and Eve in the garden (see Genesis 3:15) and then again to Abraham and his Seed (see Genesis 13:16; 15:5, and also Romans 4:13 and then Galatians 3:15 -17 in the Weymouth Translation)

Now Abraham's Seed is Christ; thus the initial Covenant was actually made *to Christ Himself,* in the eternal ages past, from before the ages. (See Ephesians 1:4 & 5)

So, from before the fall, from way back in the beginning when the thought of Man was first formed, **there was a decree made within God, there was an agreement established between the Father and the Son, a covenant made concerning Man; an eternal unbreakable decree, <u>before the ages</u>** (see 1 Corinthians 2:7).

That is why the prophets could so boldly speak and prophesy of the coming Lamb (see 1 Peter 1:19 & 20, and Revelation 13:8), *"...**the Lamb that was slain from before the foundations of the world; <u>from before time even began</u>**."*

So, just like the Law given by Moses could not annul or abrogate that Abrahamic Covenant, *in the same way,* the agreement and legal contract made between Adam and the devil **cannot annul or abrogate that agreement,** *that **covenant**, that promise of deliverance, that legal contract, that ETERNAL document, preserved in Christ **and then revealed and reintroduced in the fullness of time**.*

*Christ, being our **new and yet eternal** legal document from of old, **trumps and cancels** that other legal agreement between Adam and the devil.*

*That document that stood against us, that letter of accusation; the accuser of the brethren, the father of lies' own contract **of deception** has been canceled.*

But let's get back to Hebrews Chapter 2 now, reading again from Verse 10.

Hebrews 2:10,

10 *"...**For it was fitting, that He,** for whom and by whom all things exist, **in bringing many sons to glory**,"*

*"...that He should make **the pioneer** of **their salvation** perfect through suffering..."*

*He made **our salvation** perfect through suffering. **He perfected, or completed our salvation through His suffering.***

11 *"...For **both He** who sanctifies **and those** who are sanctified* (by His suffering; by His work of redemption);"

*"…For **both He** who sanctifies **and those** who are sanctified **are all OUT OF ONE**"* it says literally in the Greek.

2 Corinthians 5:18,

18 *"…**All this is from God**, who through Christ, reconciled **the world** to Himself…"*

And now Hebrews 2:11 continues on to say,

11 *"…For **both He** …and they …**ARE ALL OUT OF ONE**,"*

*"…**this is why He is not ashamed to call them BRETHREN.**"*

1 Peter 4:1-5 says,

1 *"**Therefore,** since Christ suffered **FOR US**, IN THE FLESH, **arm yourselves** also **with the same mind**, for he who has (meaning **we** who have, in Him) suffered in the flesh, (that person) **has ceased from sin.**"*

*…Thus, **all of us,** in Him, **in His suffering in the flesh,** have ceased from sin.*

'Wait a minute, Peter. We did not suffer in the flesh…'

No, but **He did! *We suffered with Him* in His death. His death *was OUR death!***

He suffered *for us* IN THE FLESH, that <u>WE</u> *may be set free IN THE FLESH!*

2 *"...so that he (we, meaning every single individual) no **longer should live THE REST OF HIS (OUR) TIME IN THE FLESH for the lusts of men, BUT FOR THE WILL OF GOD.***"

3 *"**For we have spent enough of our past lifetime in doing the will of the gentiles—** when we walked in licentiousness* (giving ourselves a license to do whatever we wanted to, whatever we walked in at any given time) *...when we walked in **lusts*** (strong but rather empty passions of all kinds, mainly self-centered greed and sexual perversions, but also things like), *drunkenness, revelries, drinking parties, and abominable idolatries* (all kinds of perverse addictions)*."*

4 *"In regard to these things, they think it strange that you do not run with them in the same flood of dissipation anymore* (giving themselves over to destructive behaviors), *speaking evil of you."*

5 *"(Whether they realize it or not)* **they are accountable to Him** (they owe Him their very existence) **who has already judged the living and the dead."**

The apostle Paul says in Romans 1:18,

18 *"For God already revealed His displeasure from heaven (in the Law), against all ungodliness and unrighteousness of Men,* **WHO SUPPRESS THE TRUTH in unrighteousness."**

The Ruach Translation says,

*"…(The Law) revealed and expressed God's grievance from heaven against all unrighteousness and ungodliness, **because Mankind foolishly suppressed and concealed the truth in their unrighteousness**, even though God is not a stranger to anyone, **for what can be known of God is already manifest in them**."*

Paul goes on to say in Chapter 2:5,

5 "…in accordance with YOUR HARDNESS of heart, your HARDENED and IMPENITRANT hearts (in other words your stubbornness) **you are treasuring up for yourselves WRATH** (you live your life in self-destruct mode under your own judgment) **in (spite of) the day of wrath and revelation of the righteous judgment of God (which already took place in Christ),"** *…in other words:* **…in (spite of) the fact that God has already judged you as righteous in Christ!**

6 "…who 'will render (…who has already rendered) *to each one according to his deeds* (according to their individual preference and personal choice),'"* Paul was merely referencing a prophetic Scripture from the past which was now fulfilled in Christ.

He says, *"God will render …or grant …or give …to each one, **according to their own passion …according to the passion of their heart!**"*

7 *"**eternal life, to those** who by patient continuance in doing good **seek for glory, honor, and immortality;"***

8 *"...but to those who are self-seeking* (instead of God-seeking) *AND **DO NOT OBEY THE TRUTH,** but obey unrighteousness – they will reap their own destruction, their own indignation and wrath.* (They will continue to live their lives in self-destruct mode under their own judgment),*"*

9 *"...tribulation and anguish, ON EVERY SOUL OF MAN who does evil..."*

(God doesn't bring about this *tribulation and anguish.* They bring it on themselves. Evil still pays its own wage. Evil in Greek is the word *PANEROS,* which means: Hardship, labors, toil, annoyances, and frustration)

He goes on to say in Verse 10,

10 *"...but glory, honor, and peace TO EVERYONE WHO WORKS WHAT IS GOOD..."*

And then in Verse 11 he says,

11 *"For **there is no partiality with God."***

The Mirror Bible in Romans 2:4-16 says it so much more beautifully and puts it this way:

4 *"**No one can afford to get the wrong idea about God's goodness 2; He hates sin but***

loves Man! The wealth of His benevolence 2 and His resolute 3 refusal to let go of us in His patient 4 passion is to shepherd 5 everyone into a radical 1 change of mind. (It is the revelation of the goodness of God that leads us to repentance 1 [to a radical change of mind]! Paul often has to remind his readers that his emphasis on the goodness of God is not a cheap excuse for them to continue in sin [see 6:1]. The word, **chrestotetos 2,** from **chraomai** meaning: to receive a loan; life is on loan to us as it were. Life is God's property, and **anoches 3** comes from **ana**, which shows intensity and echo. It means: to hold, or embrace, as in echo. The word, **makrothumias 4** means: to be patient in bearing the offenses and injuries of others. Literally, passion that goes a long way; from the root word **thuo**, to slay a sacrifice. The word, **ago 5** means: to lead as a shepherd leads his sheep. The word "repentance" is a fabricated word from the Latin, penance, and to give religion even more mileage, the English word became re-penance! That is not what the Greek word means at all! The word, **metanoia 1,** comes from **meta,** meaning: together with, and **nous,** meaning: mind, thus, together with God's mind. The word suggests a radical 1 mind shift; to return to one's right mind. [See Isa 55:8-10])

5 *"A calloused heart that resists change accumulates cause to self-destruction, while God's righteous judgment* (that Christ bore) *is already revealed in broad daylight."*

6 *"**By resisting Him, you are on your own; your own deeds will judge you.** (Rejecting His goodness [mentioned in verse 4] keeps you snared in the illusion of a sin-consciousness and inevitable condemnation.)"*

7 *"**The quest of Mankind is to be constant in that which is good, glorious and honorable, and of imperishable value. We are eager to pursue the original blueprint-life of the ages 1.** (The life of the ages, from **aionios** 1, which is the most attractive life we could possibly live, it is the life of our design, yet it remains elusive outside of the redemption that Christ achieved on our behalf. Not even the most sincere decision to live a blameless life under the law or any sincere philosophy could measure up to the heart hunger of humanity.)"*

8 *"**Yet there are those who ignore the truth through unbelief 2.** (The truth about their original identity as sons) **They continue to exist as mere hirelings 1, motivated by a monthly wage** (rather than sonship). **They believe in their failure and unrighteousness and are consumed by outbursts of anger and displeasure.** (The word, **eithea** 1, comes from **erithos,** working as a hireling for wages; often translated self-willed or contentious. The word, **apeitheo** 2, means: to be not persuaded, without faith, often wrongly translated as to be disobedient.)"*

9 *"**Pressures from every side, like an overcrowded room 1,** (or a cramped foot in an*

88

undersized shoe,) **is the experience of the soul of everyone who does what is worthless. The fact that the Jews are Jewish does not make their experience of evil any different from that of the Greeks.** *(Symptoms of disease are the same in anyone; they are not a respecter of persons. The word,* **stenochoria** *1 means: narrowness of room.)"*

10 **"In sharp contrast to this, bliss, self-worth and total tranquility is witnessed by everyone, both Jew and Greek, who finds expression in that which is good. We are tailor-made for good.**"

11 **"God does not judge people on face value.**"

12 **"Ruin and self-destruction are the inevitable results of sin, whether someone knows the Law or not.**"

13 **"Righteousness is not a hearsay-thing. It is faith-inspired practical living, giving new definition to the Law.**"

14 **"For even a pagan's natural instinct will confirm the Law to be present in his conscience even though he has never heard about Jewish laws. Thus, he proves to be a law unto himself.**"

15 **"The Law is so much more than a mere written code, its presence in human conscience even in the absence of the**

*written instruction is obvious, condemning
or commending personal conduct.*"

16 "*Every hidden, conflicting thought will
be disclosed in the daylight of God's
scrutiny, based on the good news of Jesus
Christ that I proclaim.* (*The ineffectiveness of
good intentions and self-discipline to produce
lasting change will be exposed as worthless in
contrast to the impact of the message of
Christ's death and resurrection as representing
mankind's death and new birth as our ultimate
reference to our redeemed identity and
innocence.).*"

Now I am saying all this here in this book, and I
will probably say it again in other books, **to
establish and lay a foundation for your
Christian faith:**

**It is a fact that in the mind and the opinion
of God,** *redemption is a reality.* **It is a
settled reality!**

God is not in the process of deciding about
Man's release. *He decreed and declared
Man's release before the ages,* **and in His
Son,** *God exhibits and secures our release.*

That release belongs to **whoever will
embrace it** *by believing in the success of the
work of redemption. It belongs to* **whoever
has a heart to believe these things!** It
belongs to whoever will embrace that
release by agreeing with God!

*That release from the Fall and all its consequences ...**that release** into everything God decreed concerning Man from before time began **belongs to all of us!***

That release belongs to us all** because He promised it **and gave it to us** in Christ Jesus, and **He accomplished it in the work of Redemption!

That release and restoration of our original design <u>truly</u> belongs to us all! It is for whosoever <u>believes it and embraces it</u>!

*"...**there is no partiality with God!***"

That is why I also cannot settle for or accept the doctrine of predestination **the way it has been taught** in many circles of the so called *"Church"* for many years ...you know, that doctrine that says that *God includes some, while excluding others,* that God has predestined some for salvation, and He has predestined others not to be saved!

I truly believe that doctrine to be nothing other than *a doctrine of demons that has infiltrated the religious "Church,"* for it undermines *the very heart of the Gospel.* It undermines *everything the Gospel stands for. It is an insult to Christ's work of redemption.* It is, in fact, nothing short of blasphemy, **because it opposes the very father-heart of God, the very love-nature of God, *who desires that none should be lost.***

2 Timothy 2:4,

4 *"...who desires all men to be saved;"*

God desires all to be saved!

"...He desires all men to come to the knowledge of the TRUTH!"

Listen, I say again: **God decreed and declared *Man's release* before the ages, *and God exhibits and secures that release in His Son.***

...And so He says to us, He says to YOU, *'BELIEVE IT AND EMBRACE IT FULLY!'*

He desires ALL of Mankind to be saved, *to be rescued,* to fully come into that release, *by coming to the knowledge of the truth!*

Let me tell you the story of a black eagle:

After ten years of captivity, a black eagle was released from the Pretoria zoo in South Africa. In South Africa there are some beautiful mountains. The nature conservationist told my friends, Francois and Lydia du Toit, of how this eagle was brought to them to be released again after so many years of captivity, and how excited they were as they anticipated this beautiful bird soaring up in the sky after its release. *But they were so disappointed when this bird would not realize its release.* They got it out of the cage, but there it sat. In its mind, it would not allow itself to see beyond those bars of yesterday. You know, that bird was never created to be caged; it was never designed for that. It just sat there, *and yet it was free.*

The conservationist continued to tell my friends how, after a few hours, another black eagle began to circle in that area, and as soon as the eagle that was now released from captivity saw the other one, *there was a reflection, a knowledge communicated by its flight.*

When the once captive eagle heard the voice of the free eagle, it just took off and joined the other one in flight, and they began to circle together in the sky; i*n that unrestricted living-space.*

And that, my friend, is the Gospel. You see nothing we can do, *can add to our identity.* You don't become a new creation, *you ARE a new creation.* **We can only discover and believe these things, *but we cannot add to them.* We cannot add to what God says we already are, *we can only discover it and live it.* We can only discover our true selves, *and be ourselves!***

I say again: **Nothing you do can add to who you are!** Discover your true self in Christ Jesus, *and be that person you discover there!*

Nothing you do can add to your liberty!

You cannot become more free, more set apart, more sanctified, more redeemed,

more righteous, than what He says you already are!

Ephesians 2:8 & 9,

8 *"...**For by grace** <u>you</u> **have been saved** <u>through faith</u>, *and **that** not of yourselves; **it is a gift of God**,"*

9 *"...**<u>not of works, lest anyone should boast</u>***..."*

It's a faith thing from beginning to end. It's a gift from God.

You either *see* it, or you don't. You either *believe* it or you don't! It's that simple!

1 Corinthians 1:30,

30 *"...**<u>Of God are you in Christ</u>**,"*

*"...whom God made **to be our wisdom**."*

*"...**our righteousness**;"*

*"...**our sanctification**;"*

*"...**our redemption**."*

And He just calls us in the Gospel, by the truth of the Gospel, *to see Jesus, not as an excuse for lack in our lives, but we see Jesus as the One who displays our worth, our liberty, our identity, <u>everything.</u> amen!?*

Father, we thank you that we may behold the glory of God *in the face of Christ,* **as in a mirror, and _beholding Him_ we are being changed, _instantly,_ as revelation dawns on us!**

I thank you Father, that during these days, and also in this book, *you are drawing every individual* **into a new gazing,** **a new beholding of Him, in the** _mirror_ **of your Word!**

And as we behold, *we are* _changed_**!**

And we're not going *to interfere with that change,* we're not going to try, with personal effort, to speed up, or add to, that change, because we in ourselves cannot *bring about that change* **which You are the author of.**

You are the author of that change *through our* **seeing,** *through our* **beholding, and embracing, and believing,** **that which was from the beginning.**

That which was from the beginning, we have now also **heard;** we have now also **seen.** Our own spiritual eyes **have looked upon it** and **our faith hands have handled** *that which concerns* **that Word of Life!**

And we thank You that *that life* _was made manifest_**!**

Father, that Word, that life, *was manifested,* and we're not interested here in these days, *to be entertained* with theology and doctrine, *and human opinion. But we have a hunger and* **an interest for the light to be made manifest,** <u>in us also</u>!

We bear witness and testify to it, to this KOINONIA, *this fellowship,* **this transforming relationship with your Word, with the gospel of God, with Jesus, with the Spirit of Christ Himself!**

We bear witness and testify to **this transformation taking place, and this partaking of the Divine nature.**

And so right now, today, we lift up our eyes *and we* **see** *the harvest.* **It's white, it's ready, in Jesus name**.

Thank you Father!

Father, I thank you that **the** *truth* **of your Word, the truth of the gospel,** *settles in our hearts, and nourishes our thinking,* **and imparts life there, as You combine Spirit with spirit**, *in Jesus' name!*

Amen.

Praise you Lord!

Now, I know sometimes when I write and I teach it may sound real heavy. You know, I mean, it's a Big Word. *I know it's a deep revelation, and you might think it's too hard to grasp,* **but I don't want you to limit your**

ability to receive to how entertained you _felt_ while reading this book.

Sometimes the message comes across in a lighter, funnier way, and people laugh and carry on and have an enjoyable time, and they're all happy and everything. But sometimes the Word comes across more seriously, more soberly. _And I don't want you to limit the effect of the Word_ **to how you were able to register and respond in your senses.**

God wants to take us beyond an experience that lasts only as long as the goose-bumps last.

He wants to communicate a substance _that is of ETERNAL weight,_ a substance that is _everlasting,_ so it can take you and carry you _right through your next crisis!_ And that substance is TRUTH! God's eternal TRUTH!

Did you know that you are going to face some real crises in your life, some real severe challenges, contradictions, and storms that beat against your little house?

But your house is as sure as the rock is, **because we're built upon a sure foundation**, _amen!?_

So in these days, the times may even grow worse, **but we're just going to keep looking unto that rock from which we were hewn, the quarry from which we were dug,** and thus, like living stones ourselves, *we are going to be built* **together, *established* together, *settled* together, *even* cemented together, *in our union with Him, and one another.***

Chapter 8

Love Will Undo A Multitude Of Sins

If you are not currently part of a **true** Christian family of believers, just ask God and He will lead you and help you get connected with other Christians *who believe and live by these redemption truths and new creation realities.* God wants you to *make friends with them* and to fellowship with them *in the truth.* Ask Him to connect you with those who have understood the grace of God in full, and who have also therefore been fully immersed in the indwelling Holy Spirit, and can flow with Him in the gifts of the Spirit, like speaking in other tongues and so forth, *just like the believers you read about in the book of Acts. Oh yes, these things are real, and they are for today!*

These precious believers, once you find them, and they embrace you warmly and welcome you into their friendship circle and family, will love you and share with you *and help you get fully immersed in redemption realities, and the things of the Holy Spirit.* You can fully expect them to love you like family, and be there for you, and encourage you, as you grow fully into this new creation you already are. And if they don't embrace you and love you passionately like a warm and genuinely loving family, **then get away from them as fast as you can.**

I'm serious, run as far away from them as you can! **Not everything that carries the Christian label is genuine, there are a lot of religious fakes out there, who, even though they may sound legit, they do not have a clue what they are talking about when it comes to real redemption realities, and therefore they cannot walk in the genuine love of God!** That's why I say you need to make this a matter of genuinely trusting Father God to lead you, and even then, you might still run into some snakes!

But I am not saying this to try and discourage you from looking for and wanting to be a part of something genuine! God knows many of us have had enough of living a love-less life in this world! I cannot emphasize enough how vital it is for you to develop <u>real</u> relationships with genuine BELIEVERS who TRULY UNDERSTAND REDEMPTION REALITIES in order to become a part of the extended family of God <u>in a genuine way</u>.

Satan is always trying to cause division through the breakdown of <u>real</u> relationships.

If he can get you unattached and isolated, he can shut you down and keep you from being fruitful and effective in the things of God.

I mean, you might still bear some small little fruit in your life, but God is interested in that fruit increasing; He is interested in much fruit, and fruit which remain!

Remember this,

"...two are better than one and a threefold cord is not easily broken."

In fact, Ecclesiastes 4:9-12 says,

9 *"Two are better than one, because they have a good reward for their labor."*

10 *"For if they fall, one will lift up his companion."*

"But woe to him who is alone when he falls, for he has no one to help him up."

11 *"Again, if two lie down together, they will keep warm; but how can one be warm alone?"*

12 *"Though one may be overpowered by another, two can withstand him."*

"...and (three is even better than two) a threefold cord is not quickly broken."

Jesus said that the world would come to know Him **by the love we have.** It is His desire for us to walk in unity, and together, *"have a good reward for our labor."* ...In other words, *make a difference in this world we live in.*

As far as it is up to you, *walk in love and forgiveness towards everyone.*

1 Peter 4:8-11,

8 *"And **above all, <u>hold unfailing</u> your love for one another,** since 'Love covers a multitude of sins…"*

It's one thing to love one another when everything feels right, but God is calling us to walk in the Ephesians 4 kind of love, *which will overcome all challenges in our relationships with one another.*

God is compelling us *"to do everything in our might…"* - Ephesians 4:3,

3 *"…**to preserve the unity of the spirit, in the bond of peace**…"*

That means *I need to walk in forgiveness.*

Ephesians 4:2,

2 *"…**forbearing one another <u>and truly, genuinely, loving one another</u>**…"*

1 Peter 4:8-11,

8 *"And **above all, <u>hold unfailing</u> your love for one another,** since 'Love covers a multitude of sins…"*

*"…<u>**unfailing**</u>…"*

Let me tell you, love is not keen to listen to the next story and talk about the next bit of gossip about somebody else. **Let's stop that sort of conversation in our lives and in our fellowship with one another.**

'Love covers…'

Verse 9,

9 *"…**Practice** (become skilled at) hospitality <u>ungrudging</u> towards one another…"*

God wants to produce in us a quality in our hospitality: *"…**ungrudging**…"*

That means we have to <u>open</u> our hearts *and then our homes,* and <u>invite people in</u> *and become skilled at it.*

Romans 15:1-2,

1 *"**We who are strong ought to bear** with the failings of the weak and not to please ourselves."*

2 *"Let each one of us please his neighbor for his good **to <u>edify</u> him** (not just to put up with him)."*

To *"**<u>edify</u>**"* means to use the Word, the truth of the gospel, to **IMPART STRENGTH** to the weak one. You see, we could so easily avoid the weak and say, *'They're too weak to fellowship with.'* **But God wants to instill in us His sense of responsibility, *because of*** *love.* **Therefore, make an effort** *to be sensitive to them,* **and to strengthen them.**

Paul goes on to say in Verse 3,

3 *"For even Christ did not please Himself, but as it is written, 'The reproaches of those who reproach You fell on Me.'*

Listen, **true love is a strong thing, not some wishy-washy thing. To love and accept a person** *does not mean we are to condone their sin.* We are to love people <u>enough</u> *to see them totally released from the sin that is destroying their lives <u>and to help bring that breakthrough about</u>!*

If we don't use the truth of redemption *and the immense love of God in our hearts for them to rescue them from self-destruct mode,* then who will?

We have a responsibility to rescue them *because of love,* to be sensitive to them *in that way,* and that means: *to strengthen them; to love them and gently impart strength to them with the Word of truth; the gospel of their salvation.*

Proverbs 27:5 & 6 says,

5 *"**Better is an open rebuke than hidden love.**"*

6 *"Faithful are **the wounds** of **a friend**, but the flattering kisses of an enemy are deceitful."*

You see, the love of the New Covenant does not excuse sin, **but deals with it <u>in love</u>. It wounds, *but it's a wound that brings healing.*** It's like doing a necessary surgery. It still hurts, it is still a wound, *but it is for your good: it helps you, **it saves your life.***

James 5:19 & 20,

19 *"Brethren, if anyone among you **wanders from The Truth,** and someone <u>turns him back</u>,"*

20 *"let him know that he who <u>turns</u> a sinner **from the error of his way <u>will save a soul from death</u>** (from self-destruct mode and the spiritual disconnect that is produced by it) and 'cover a multitude of sins.'"*

Galatians 6:1 & 2,

1 *"Brethren, if a man is **overtaken** <u>in any trespass</u>, you who are spiritual, **restore** (rescue) such a one **in a spirit of gentleness** (not condemnation and judgmentalism), considering yourself lest you also be tempted…"*

Lest you become puffed up in self-righteousness and pride, coming down on your brother, judging him too harshly.

*"…**restore** such a one **in a spirit of gentleness**…"*

In other words, **don't wound your brother's spirit, and put him under self-loathing and rejection and condemnation, *by being too harsh with him. But don't be too lenient either. Love's confrontation is never comfortable,* but it is an absolute must!**

2 *"**Bear** (remove, carry away) one another's burdens, and so fulfill the law of Christ."*

Our authentic design accurately dictates that we genuinely love one another. It's the only authentic life we can live. To live anything less and walk in any lesser way is to live a lie. There is no need to put up with anything fake or false within us, when we are called to a new reality! We are called to be real; to be the love nature of God our Father on display, His image, His likeness, nothing less! That's what the *"law of Christ"* is all about!

So, seeing that this is the new reality we are called to, listen carefully and take some lessons from Paul:

2 Corinthians 1:24,

24 *"**Not that we have dominion over your faith**, but we are fellow workers **for your joy**; <u>for by faith you stand.</u>"*

According to Paul in other words, **we have no dominion over one another's faith, *we are only helpers of one another's joy*.** That means: We *are not to try and manipulate and control people, with our words, to try and force* *them to do what is right, or what we think is right, or what we think they ought to do.* **But we are to try and rescue them, and strengthen them, and edify them, with the Word, with the gospel,** *with the truth of redemption,* **if indeed** they wander from the Truth **in a cloud of deception,** *or are overtaken by that deception in a trespass.*

But when all is said and done, *they either stand by their own faith or they don't.* It's as simple as that. Our faith and love can encourage and challenge them, *and impart strength to them,* **but ultimately they cannot stand on our faith.** *They can only* stand *on their own faith.*

Colossians 3:12 & 13,

12 *"Therefore,* as God's own chosen people, holy and beloved, *put on tender mercies, kindness, humbleness of mind* (not being self-righteous, or thinking too much of yourself), *put on meekness* (yielding yourself to the Word and the voice of God), *and long-suffering;"*

(Being willing to suffer mistreatment from people, as you work on trying to rescue them in love, from Satan's clutches)

13 *"bearing with one another* (not only putting up with one another's idiosyncrasies or personality differences, *but strengthening each other through love, and some understanding,*

and with the Word, **removing and carrying away one another's burdens**);"

*"...**and forgiving one another, if anyone has a complaint (or accusation) against another; <u>even as Christ forgave you</u>, so you also must do**."*

Ephesians 4:32,

32 *"**And be <u>kind</u> to one another, tenderhearted,** <u>forgiving</u> one another, **<u>just as God in Christ also forgave you</u>**"*

Matthew 18:21-35,

21 *"Then Peter came to Jesus and said, **"How often shall my brother sin against me, and I forgive him?** Up to seven times?"*

22 *"Jesus said to him, 'I do not say to you, up to seven times, **but rather seventy times seven**.'*

23 *"Therefore...* (In other words: Let me tell you a parable to explain what I mean, *because, contrary to what you might be thinking Peter,* **what I just said is <u>not</u> too big for you to comprehend <u>and walk in</u>, *and I really want you to get the point of what I'm saying*.** So let me tell you this parable, and maybe you'll get the point then,)

*"...the Kingdom of Heaven **is like** a certain king who wanted to settle accounts with his servants."* (In other words He is not saying that

108

this is what God is like and that this is exactly what happens in the kingdom of Heaven, but He is highlighting the principles of the kingdom by comparing the kingdom of heaven [that unseen realm within us] with what happened in this made up story)

23 *"...the Kingdom of Heaven **is like** a certain king who wanted to settle accounts with his servants."*

24 *"And when he had begun to settle accounts, one was brought to him who owed him ten thousand talents."*

25 *"But as he was not able to pay, his master commanded that he be sold, with his wife and children and all that he had, and that payment be made."*

26 *"The servant therefore fell down before him saying, '**Master, have patience with me, and I will pay you all**.'*

27 *"Then the master of that servant was moved with compassion, **released the man, and forgave him the debt.**"*

28 *"**But** that servant **went out and found one of his fellow servants who owed him a hundred denarii** (a fairly large amount, like 3 month's salary, but still a very minuscule amount in comparison to ten thousand talents) **and he laid hands on him and grabbed him by the throat, saying, 'Pay me what you owe!'**

Why did he do that? I believe it was because he still wanted to somehow justify himself before the king, through his own efforts. He still wanted to pay the master back, even if it was in installments, even if the first installment was only 3 months' worth of salary for the average man. **He still couldn't accept forgiveness and forgive himself and let go of it, _and so it limited him in his love walk_.**

You see, **if you begin to think that that is the way your God still looks at you,** _you are going to feel justified in looking at others the same way and treating them just as harshly._

Jesus continues,

29 _"So his fellow servant **fell down at his feet and begged him, saying, 'Have patience with me, and I will pay you all.'**_

30 _"**And he would not**, but went and threw him into prison till he should pay the debt."_

31 _"So when his fellow servants saw what had been done, **they were very grieved**, and came and told their master all that had been done."_

32 _"Then this king and master, after he had called the man, said to him, '**You wicked servant! _I forgave you all that debt_ because you begged me."_

33 *"Should you not also have had compassion and mercy on your fellow servant, just as I had pity on you?'*

34 *"And his master the king was angry. He delivered the man up to the tormentors* (torturers) *until he should pay <u>all that was due</u>."*

Even until recently, I used to read this portion of Scripture and get all condemned myself, *and somehow relate this to Father God,* and think, *'Well there you have it, the King got so angry that He revoked His forgiveness and this man is now going to be delivered up to the tormentors to be tortured forever in Hell.'*

But there has always been something that bothered me about this Scripture. *It never quite made sense to me.* For instance: *Why throw a man in prison if you want him to repay his debt?* I mean, if a man is in prison, *how is he going to be able to work and repay the debt? And what on earth is torturing the man going to accomplish?* I mean, *torturing is not going to get the debt paid; only putting the man to work is going to get your money back.*

So, recently, while I was reading this Scripture the Holy Spirit opened my eyes to something I never saw before. He began to break open new revelation in my spirit and showed me that *there is so much more which the Father is trying to communicate to my spirit than what the casual observer can see.*

111

He began to reveal to me afresh *the heart of the Father.* He began to talk to me about, *"… all that was due."*

So let me ask you the same question He asked me: **How much was due?**

NOTHING!

Why? **Because when His master forgave him the debt, *he forgave it all.***

So really, if you think of it, *the king wanted this man to grasp something.* **He didn't actually want to torture the man.** What the king was saying is that **this man within himself, within his conscience, within his inner-man, in his heart and in his spirit; *he was going to be tormented there, until he was willing to accept his forgiveness.***

Only then could he personally say to the tormentors himself, *'Hey listen guys; **you can stop tormenting me now, because the debt was canceled.** I was forgiven the debt entirely, and therefore have a legal right to go free without suffering any more torment from you!'*

And they would have to let him go *because he was and is legally a free man.*

Remember, even though the master got strongly disappointed *and his anger flared up at this man,* **in his love for this man and for the other servant's worth,** he never did say,

112

'I revoke my forgiveness.'

Another thing I also want you to notice is that the king did not go and release the other man who was thrown in prison. No, it was up to this servant number one, **to accept his own forgiveness first, and then to go and forgive his brother, and go let him out of torment and prison as well.**

Matthew 18:35,

35 **'So My heavenly Father also will do to you if each of you, <u>from his heart</u> does not forgive his brother his trespasses."**

"…from his heart…"

See, this will affect your love walk **because it is a heart issue!**

*"…***So My heavenly Father also will do to you***…"*

*"…***He delivered the man up to the tormentors***…"*

God gave all of us a sensitive conscience, and thus it is not God, but your conscience that will torment you! *Your conscience will be tormented* **in self-righteousness** (trying to be justified by the merits of your own efforts), *because as long as you rely on your own self-righteousness* **you will always stand guilty and accused in your own heart.**

Can you see that? Can you see that, Self-righteousness, _not God,_ will torment your conscience! And that sin *will mar your blameless, innocent, fellowship with God,* and your stance before others. *It will rob you, and it will keep you from enjoying true intimacy in your fellowship with your Father.*

Don't even try to fool yourself in this: The sin of self-righteousness, and the inevitable self-condemnation that follows, as self-punishment for that sin, **will prevent you from experiencing total, complete intimacy with your Father. You will suddenly notice that there is something missing, *that you lost something between you and God in your personal private times with Him,*** and the *intimacy you experience is not as deep as it used to be as you try to fellowship with Him.*

You will find yourself **drawing back while you are trying to draw near!**

You will find a separation from your Father's sweet fellowship, **and be tormented and suffer this way until you let go of that thing,** and release your brother from his guilt according to Matthew 18:35 that we just read.

Jesus said these things, not me!

You would do well to go and read 1 Corinthians 13. The whole chapter is devoted to walking in love. And don't do window-shopping when you read it either, thinking that you can never become like that and that the best you can
114

hope for is that this is what we will be like one day in Heaven.

NO! This is who you are, right now, already. It's not who you are going to become someday. Remember: YOU *ARE* A <u>NEW</u> CREATION *NOW*!

Romans 12:1 & 2,

1 *"I beseech you therefore brethren, by* (in view of) *the mercies of God, **that you present your bodies a living sacrifice, holy*** (exclusively set apart in your love, only for what He has purposed for you)**, *acceptable to God, which is your **reasonable** service*** (It is only logical, not unreasonable)*."*

2 *"...And do not be **conformed*** (that means pressured into a mold, shaped, manipulated into being something you are not)*;"*

*"...And do not be conformed **to this world*** (and the way they think)*, but be <u>**transformed**</u>..."*

He is referring to the process of metamorphosis by which a caterpillar is changed into a butterfly.

Note that the caterpillar was always meant to become a butterfly. ***In fact, that caterpillar <u>always was</u> a butterfly.***

Its <u>true nature</u> came forth in the metamorphosis.

James 1:18,

18 *"…Of His own will He* **brought us forth** *by the Word of TRUTH…"*

We too believed The Truth and were **"brought forth" as faith was birthed in our hearts.**

John 8:36,

36 *"…Whom the Son* **sets free** *is free indeed."*

Romans 12:2,

2 *"…And do not be conformed to this world, but* **be transformed** **by the renewing of your** **mind***, that you may prove* (taste and experience for yourself) *what is that good, acceptable, perfect, will of God."*

*"…***Be transformed by the renewing of your** **mind,** *that you may* **prove***…"*

Not just taste and experience for yourself, *but also be able to accurately present and make known these redemption truths,* **to preach it** **and show it forth through your life to the** **world***, to reveal to them in clarity,*

"…what the will of God is."

So that through encountering your life and your strong and clear witness and testimony, God's will may become *"good, acceptable, and perfect,"* to them also.

In closing, **We are to love people, *by helping them get free from the sin that is destroying their lives.* That means doing everything we can to make the truth of the Word known to them, *in its full implications,* with clarity, *and so to rescue them with the Word of Truth.***

I urge you to get yourself a copy of *"The Mirror Bible,"* it is the best paraphrase translation of the Scriptures from the original Greek that I have ever read, and it's available online at: www.amazon.com and several other book sellers.

If you want me or someone a part of our team to come to where you are, *anywhere in the world,* and give a talk or teach you and some of your friends *about the gospel message and these redemption realities,* simply contact us at www.livingwordintl.com …or you can always find me on www.facebook.com

If your life has changed as a result of reading this book, *please write to me and let me know.*

I would love to share in your joy,

…so that my joy in writing this series of books may be full!

"That which was from the beginning,

which we have heard
(with our spiritual ears),
which we have seen
(with our spiritual eyes),
which we have looked upon
(beheld, focused our attention upon),
and which our hands have also handled
(which we have also experienced),

concerning the Word of life,

*119

we declare to you,

that you also may have this
fellowship with us;

and truly our fellowship is with
the Father
and with His Son Jesus Christ.

And these things we write to you
that your joy may be full."

- 1John 1:1-4

About the Author

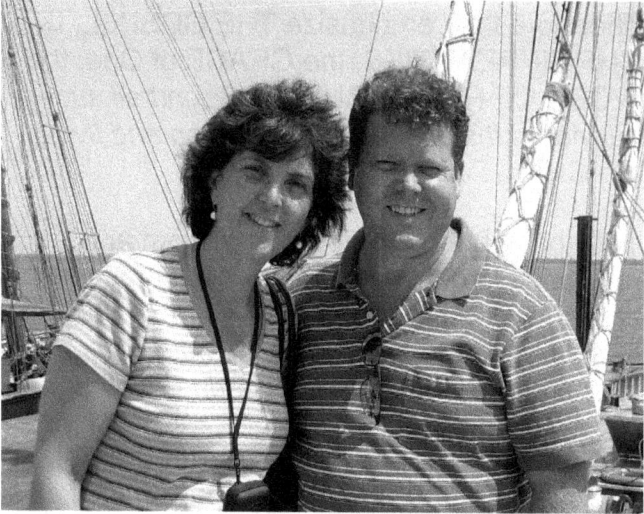

Rudi & Carmen Louw named their ministry: Living Word International, because they love to travel and minister, both locally and internationally.

Rudi was born and raised in the country of South Africa, while Carmen grew up in Cortland, New York.

They function in the ministry of reconciliation (2 Corinthians 5:18-21) and flow strongly with the Holy Spirit and His anointing to teach, preach, prophesy, heal, and whatever is needed to touch people's lives with the reality of God's love and power.

God has given them keen insight into what He has to say to mankind in the work of redemption *concerning the revelation and restoration of humanity's true identity.*

Therefore they emphasize THE GOSPEL, IN CHRIST REALITIES, the GRACE of God, the WORD OF RIGHTEOUSNESS, *and all such eternal truths essential to salvation and living the CHRIST-LIFE.*

They have been granted this wisdom and revelation into the knowledge of God by the resurrected Spirit of Jesus Christ, *to establish and strengthen believers in the faith of God, and to activate them in ministering to others.*

Not only are people set free from the poison and bondage of sin, condemnation and all kinds of intimidation, (upheld, strengthened and reinforced by age old religious ideas born out of ignorance) **but many are brought into a closer more intimate relationship with Father God, as Daddy**, through accurate teaching and unveiling of the gospel message, prophetic words, healings and miracles.

Rudi & Carmen are closely knitted together with many other effective Christians, church fellowships, and groups of believers who share the same revelation and passion **to impart the truth of the gospel to others, so as to impact and transform the world we live in with the LOVE and POWER of God.**

www.ingramcontent.com/pod-product-compliance
Lightning Source LLC
Chambersburg PA
CBHW071136090426
42736CB00012B/2131